THE BASIC COOK BOOK

Deliciously easy, every day

thermomix

Welcome

DEAR THERMOMIX™ CUSTOMER,

On behalf of Vorwerk International I wish you a warm welcome to the world of Thermomix™.

You have just purchased your Thermomix™ and I want to thank you for your trust in our brand. Thermomix™ will be your reliable assistant in the kitchen, handling all the tasks of weighing, mixing, chopping, kneading, blending, cooking and much more... without additional accessories.

Your Thermomix™ comes with *The Basic Cookbook* containing essential recipes to simplify everyday cooking. You will discover how easy it is to make fast, healthy and delicious meals for your family as well as entire effortless and all-round pleasure menus for your guests.

All of our recipes are developed and tested according to the highest quality standards. Our aim is to bring state of the art simplicity to cooking: this is why we combine traditional cooking culture with the ease of the digital lifestyle. All recipes in *The Basic Cookbook* are digitalised on the companion to your Thermomix™, the Thermomix™ recipe chip. Attach the Thermomix™ recipe chip to your Thermomix™, scroll through your recipes on the touchscreen and take advantage of the step-by-step instructions and presettings. Never has cooking been more intuitive or taken less time!

Enjoy discovering the world of culinary possibilities offered by your Thermomix™ and enjoy cooking!

My best regards,

Dirk Reznik
CEO Division Thermomix™

Table of contents

My world of Thermomix™

Thermomix™ comes with world class services for unique experiences.
For more information about our services visit us at www.thermomix.com

ADVISOR SUPPORT
PERSONALISED FOLLOW-UP

Your advisor is available to answer questions and offer support regarding every aspect of Thermomix™ and its related services.

COOKING CLASS ACADEMY
OUR EXPERIENCE AT YOUR SERVICE

Attend our cooking classes and be inspired to use your Thermomix™ daily. Enjoy this unique experience, discover new recipes and get special tips from our experts.

COOKBOOKS AND THERMOMIX™
RECIPE CHIPS

THE PERFECT PARTNERS FOR EASY COOKING

Discover our cookbook library with fantastic new recipes.
To take advantage of guided cooking just attach the
Thermomix™ recipe chip to the appliance and start
cooking. Obtain more information from your advisor.

Thermomix™:
all in one and one for all!

Here is a brief overview of your Thermomix™ to help you get started. Please refer to the instruction manual for a more comprehensive presentation of Thermomix™ features.

Varoma

Use the Varoma to steam food and to cook multiple dishes simultaneously. The Varoma consists of three parts: the Varoma dish and the Varoma lid must always be used when steaming, whereas the Varoma tray is an optional insert.

Measuring cup

The measuring cup closes the hole in the mixing bowl lid. Remove to allow more steam evaporation (replace it with the simmering basket) or when using the Varoma.

Butterfly whisk

Use the butterfly whisk for whipping and whisking (e.g. cream, egg whites). Use on speeds 🥄 to 4 (max.)

Mixing bowl

The 2.2 litre stainless steel mixing bowl with integrated heating is where food is processed and cooked.

Mixing knife

The mixing knife stirs when used at low speeds (🥄 to 1), mixes at medium speeds (2-4), and chops at higher speeds (3-10). Use ↩ to change the rotation direction (for gentle stirring on low speeds, or shredding at higher speeds).

Thermomix™ recipe chip

The Thermomix™ recipe chip carries your digital recipes and allows you to display them on your Thermomix™.

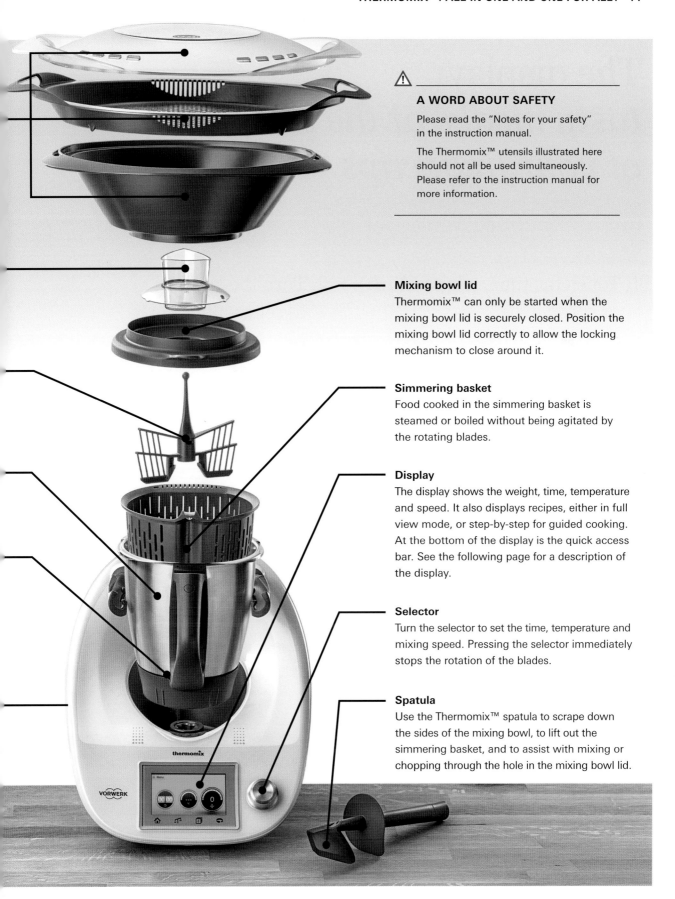

⚠

A WORD ABOUT SAFETY

Please read the "Notes for your safety" in the instruction manual.

The Thermomix™ utensils illustrated here should not all be used simultaneously. Please refer to the instruction manual for more information.

Mixing bowl lid

Thermomix™ can only be started when the mixing bowl lid is securely closed. Position the mixing bowl lid correctly to allow the locking mechanism to close around it.

Simmering basket

Food cooked in the simmering basket is steamed or boiled without being agitated by the rotating blades.

Display

The display shows the weight, time, temperature and speed. It also displays recipes, either in full view mode, or step-by-step for guided cooking. At the bottom of the display is the quick access bar. See the following page for a description of the display.

Selector

Turn the selector to set the time, temperature and mixing speed. Pressing the selector immediately stops the rotation of the blades.

Spatula

Use the Thermomix™ spatula to scrape down the sides of the mixing bowl, to lift out the simmering basket, and to assist with mixing or chopping through the hole in the mixing bowl lid.

The display:
tasty meals, at the touch of your fingertips

1. Touch the time, temperature or speed dials.

2. Turn the selector to set a value.

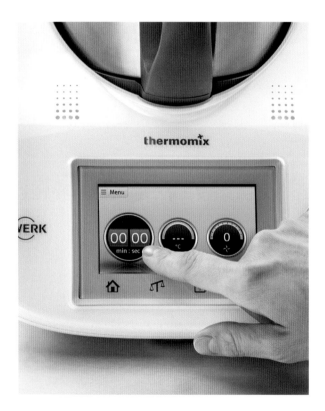

Time, temperature and speed are all displayed on one screen. The current setting is always highlighted and can easily be adjusted by turning the selector.

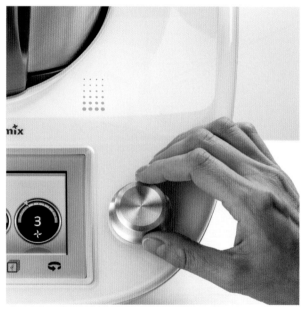

The quick access bar is always displayed.

Return to home screen

Modes (e.g. dough 🌾, turbo)

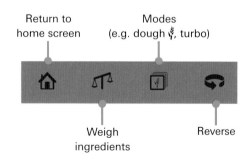

Weigh ingredients

Reverse

THERMOMIX™ RECIPE CHIP

The recipes in this cookbook are delivered on a Thermomix™ recipe chip. Further Thermomix™ recipe chips are available or will be available soon. Your advisor can help you choose and order the best ones for you.

VIEW RECIPES ON SCREEN

To view recipes, touch Menu at the top of the screen. Select a recipe and view it from beginning to end by scrolling down.

This is the same as reading the recipe from the cookbook on a digital display.

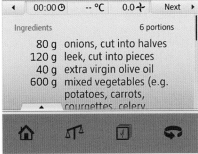

LET THE RECIPE GUIDE YOU STEP BY STEP

You can also let the recipe guide you with on-screen instructions for each step. The great advantage: time and temperature are preset for each step. All you have to do is to add the ingredients and activate the speed selector.

Touching "Next" displays the next set of instructions. Whenever you wish, you can override guided cooking instructions and adjust settings manually. You are in control!

Cooking with the Thermomix™: *the basic functions*

Having 12 functions integrated in a single kitchen appliance allows fascinating new cooking techniques. Yet all your culinary expertise can still be applied to cooking with the Thermomix™. *The main difference is that many tasks are easier and faster – as if you had an assistant in the kitchen.*

WEIGH INGREDIENTS AS YOU GO
When you add ingredients to the mixing bowl, the Thermomix™ weighs them for you, then carries on with the recipe without forgetting its settings.

THERMOMIX™ KEEPS TRACK OF THE TIME
Set a time on the Thermomix™, after which the mixing or cooking will stop. A helpful sound will inform you it is time to move on to the next step.

THE MIXING BOWL IS YOUR SAUCEPAN
The Thermomix™ mixing bowl is used for more than just mixing: it replaces your stainless steel saucepan, conducting heat efficiently to the ingredients.

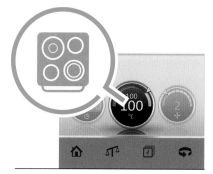

COOK IN THE MIXING BOWL
Set the target temperature to warm, heat, cook or sauté. The difference to a stove is you have total control over the temperature.

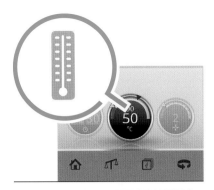

HEAT DELICATE PREPARATIONS BETWEEN 37°-95°C
Thermomix™ takes the guesswork out of heating temperature-sensitive preparations such as custards or chocolate.

STEAM FOOD IN THE VAROMA
You can steam a variety of dishes in the Varoma while cooking in your mixing bowl.

STIR ON SPEED 🥄 TO 1
To make sure ingredients cook evenly, let your Thermomix™ stir them gently for you.

MIX AND EMULSIFY ON SPEEDS 3-5
You'll soon be reaching for your Thermomix™ not just for challenging emulsions, but also for mixing simple batters and sauces. And why not, since cleaning is so easy?

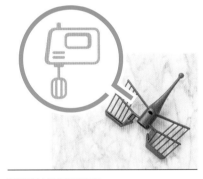

WHIP WITH THE BUTTERFLY WHISK
To whisk air into egg whites, cream or sabayon, insert the butterfly whisk on top of the mixing knife and set the speed to 2-4.

CHOP ON SPEED 4-6
With Thermomix™ you chop ingredients *after* placing them in the mixing bowl. Bear in mind that what used to take minutes will now take seconds.

BLEND ON SPEEDS 6-10
To blend, use speed 6 or higher; for a few seconds if you prefer a chunky consistency, longer for a smooth texture. When blending, always increase the speed gradually.

GRIND OR MILL ON SPEED 9-10
Grind flour from any type of grain, as well as coffee, pulses, nuts and seeds such as sesame or poppy seeds.

KNEAD USING DOUGH MODE
When making breads or pizza doughs, the dough mode imitates the kneading action of a professional baker.

Getting started with Thermomix™

The recipes in this cookbook will guide you step by step on how to use your Thermomix™. Here are some general tips that are not always mentioned in the recipes and that will help you get the most efficient use out of your Thermomix™.

Placing ingredients into a clean, dry mixing bowl ensures the best results for grinding and chopping, and is essential for whisking egg whites.

Remember to use the "tare" function. You can set the scale to zero each time you add a new ingredient.

To weigh ingredients outside the mixing bowl, tare the scale and place ingredients onto the mixing bowl lid. Or place a container onto the mixing bowl lid, tare the scale, then weigh ingredients into the container.

Always remember to insert the measuring cup, unless otherwise mentioned in a recipe.

The simmering basket can be used as a sieve, or to cover the hole in the mixing bowl lid, which allows steam to escape while helping to prevent splashing.

To emulsify sauces such as mayonnaise, very slowly pour oil onto mixing bowl lid, letting it drizzle around measuring cup in a thin stream onto rotating blades.

Make sure steam can circulate: when placing ingredients in the Varoma, leave some holes unobstructed on the sides.

Add ingredients to the simmering basket and Varoma **according to their cooking times,** placing the faster cooking ingredients (e.g. fish) on the Varoma tray.

To keep juices in the Varoma, place ingredients on a moistened sheet of baking paper, making sure a few holes remain unobstructed. For a perfect fit, trace around the Varoma tray and cut paper along the traced outline.

Use the spatula to remove the hot simmering basket as well as to scrape food out of the mixing bowl.

"With aid of spatula": when this is mentioned in a recipe, insert the Thermomix™ spatula through the hole in the mixing bowl lid, and rotate it to support the mixing and the chopping. No other spatula should be used in this way.

After emptying the mixing bowl, use the spatula, pressing it perpendicularly to the sides of the mixing bowl, to scrape out remaining ingredients. The tip of the spatula is shaped to fit around the mixing knife.

Thermomix™ is powerful. Start with a lower speed and a shorter time and check results as you go to avoid chopping ingredients too finely.

Dislodging ingredients: after emptying the mixing bowl, a few seconds on speed 10 will project residues onto the sides of the mixing bowl, making them easy to scrape out with the spatula.

Cleaning: Place water and a few drops of dishwashing liquid into the mixing bowl and mix on speed 5, touching reverse (↻) on and off a few times.

Or use a dishwasher. All Thermomix™ parts (except the main appliance and the Thermomix™ recipe chip) are dishwasher-safe.

Tips on the recipes

The Thermomix™ recipe development team is proud to present a collection of recipes that have been carefully selected and thoroughly tested. With these recipes, beginner and advanced cooks alike will learn how to use Thermomix™ by cooking delicious dishes for family and friends.

THREE TIPS TO HELP YOU ACHIEVE THE BEST RESULTS WITH THESE RECIPES

1. **Refer to the icons to help you choose a recipe**
2. **Read through the whole recipe before starting.**
3. **Use quality ingredients and prepare them before you start a recipe.**

ADAPT OUR RECIPES TO YOUR TASTE

Feel free to experiment and adapt these recipes yourself. However, bear in mind that most modifications will have an impact on the final result. For instance:

- **Temperature:** Room temperature ingredients will cook faster than refrigerated ones (e.g. eggs, milk) or frozen ingredients.
- **Fat or water content:** Substituted ingredients can have higher or lower water or fat content (e.g. tomatoes vs. red peppers, mascarpone vs. ricotta). This may impact the texture and flavour of the finished dish.
- **Size:** placing larger or smaller ingredient pieces into the mixing bowl will affect chopping, blending, and cooking times.

TIPS ON BAKING

- If the oven is not preheated, baking will take longer and may affect the finished result.
- Using a different size baking dish will affect cooking time. Cakes in smaller, deeper tins will take longer to bake than cakes in wider, shallow tins.
- The material of the baking dish — metal, ceramic, glass, silicone — also has an impact on baking time.
- Ovens vary. Insert a skewer into the middle of a cake to test whether it is cooked through: if it comes out clean, or with only a few damp crumbs attached, the cake is usually ready.
- Temperature is important in yeast-based recipes. The warmer the temperature of the room or ingredients, the faster the dough will rise. Temperatures above 45°C will kill the yeast. Cooler temperatures and longer rising times will allow more flavour to develop.
- To produce light cakes and pastries, mix batter or dough only briefly after adding the flour. Bread doughs on the other hand require more vigorous kneading.

ICONS USED IN THE RECIPES

Active time
This is the hands-on time you have to invest to prepare the recipe.

Total time
This shows the total time needed to prepare the dish until the moment it can be served. Total time also includes baking times, cooling times etc.

Difficulty
You should be able to master all the recipes without any problems. Some of them are more challenging than others, and may require more of your time if you are new to cooking.

Servings
This shows how many portions or pieces the recipe makes.

Nutritional value
The nutritional values are based on averages. The real nutritional values of your dish may differ based on the ingredients you choose.

Ingredients

TIPS ABOUT INGREDIENTS

- Always use good quality, fresh ingredients.
- The weight of ingredients in recipes refers to cleaned or peeled ingredients, where necessary. For instance, peel potatoes and onions before weighing.
- Chop herbs after washing and patting them dry with paper towels.
- To achieve uniform results, cut ingredients into evenly sized pieces (no larger than 5 cm x 5 cm).

INGREDIENTS USED IN THESE RECIPES
(unless otherwise mentioned)

- **Eggs** are European medium size (53-63 g, USA and Canada: Large).
- **Butter** is unsalted.
- **Milk** is full-fat or semi-skimmed, not fully skimmed.
- **Cream** is full fat cream (min. 30% fat), e.g. whipping or double.
- **Flour** or plain flour is white wheat flour (approx. 10-11% protein).
- For **breads and pizza dough**, use bread flour or strong flour. If none is available where you shop, plain white flour will work too.
- **Sugar** is fine white granulated sugar (caster sugar in the UK, superfine sugar in the USA), and can often be replaced with raw unrefined sugar.

- **Oil:** Use high quality first-pressed oils for salad dressings and oils with a high smoking point for frying.
- **Dry yeast** is instant yeast (which can be mixed into the recipe without rehydration).
- **Lemons** or other **citrus fruit**: zest should always be from wax-free, chemical-free fruit (organic if possible).
- **Vanilla sugar** is homemade vanilla sugar or shop-bought vanilla sugar made from natural vanilla. Synthetic vanillin can be used but the quantity must be adjusted as the flavour is sharper.
- **Canned tomatoes** are described as follows: whole (peeled), chopped (pieces visible), crushed (smooth) or tomato purée (concentrated paste).
- **"Adjust seasoning to taste"** means add salt, pepper or other seasonings to your taste.

Useful items

In addition to your Thermomix™, these are the kitchen utensils you may require for successful completion of our recipes:

- 1-2 good sharp knives
- chopping boards
- vegetable peeler
- heat-resistant cling film
- aluminium foil
- bowls of various sizes
- serving plates
- oven-proof single serving dishes such as ceramic soufflé dishes
- casserole dish
- cake tin
- loaf tin
- pastry spatula
- rolling pin
- pastry brush
- icing bag and nozzle
- biscuit cutters
- baking tray
- baking paper
- pot-holder or oven glove
- cooling rack
- wooden skewers and toothpicks
- jam jars with twist-off lids and preserving jars
- saucepans of various sizes
- frying pan
- clean kitchen towel (tea towel)
- paper towels
- scissors

Planning your week

THE BEST WAY TO BREAK THE ROUTINE IS TO PLAN AHEAD

We've all done it. We get a brand new cookbook, read through it avidly and bookmark intriguing recipes with every intention of surprising our loved ones with new and delicious dishes. But after a day's work, all we want to do is to get in and out of the shop fast. Without the cookbook on hand, we simply reach for our usual ingredients. When dinner time comes, the food we serve is quick, tried and true... but not necessarily new or exciting.

Planning ahead for your week is the best way to save time and effort while also enjoying delicious and varied menus. Trying out new recipes when you have the necessary ingredients is more fun than cooking out of habit, and the result will delight your family and friends.

When you have the ingredients on hand, cooking with Thermomix™ is pure pleasure.

A little planning turns a weeknight meal into a special occasion.

MONDAY	TUESDAY	WEDNESDAY	THURSDAY	FRIDAY	SATURDAY	SUNDAY
Smoothie		Smoothie				Pancakes + hot chocolate
Codfish with citrus butter		Risotto		Quiche Lorraine	Chopped vegetable salad	Lasagne
Spaghetti Carbonara + apple sauce	Meatballs w/ tomato sauce	Stuffed vegetables	Dinner at Elsa's: Bring dessert (chocolate mousse)	Salmon in cream sauce / Milk bread	Pizza + strawberry ice cream	

Creating a weekly menu makes it more likely you'll have all ingredients on hand when you need them.

How to adapt *your own* recipes

With 3 basic functions: time, temperature and speed, Thermomix™ performs most of the tasks required by traditional recipes.

REFER TO A SIMILAR THERMOMIX™ RECIPE

1. Get to know how Thermomix™ functions by practising with the recipes in this cookbook. Make sure you follow the safety instructions in the instruction manual when cooking in your Thermomix™.
2. Find a Thermomix™ recipe that is similar to the one you want to convert.
3. If the quality or quantities of ingredients are significantly different, adjust cooking times. Make sure you don't exceed the capacity of the mixing bowl (max. 2.2 litres).
4. Adapt the steps of the Thermomix™ recipe to your recipe. Sometimes two steps in a traditional recipe can be achieved in a single Thermomix™ step.
5. Finally, make your recipe with Thermomix™. Make notes on what works and what can be improved.

THINK "IN THERMOMIX™ MODE"

Reorganise your recipes to minimise efforts such as cleaning the mixing bowl. For instance:

Dry to wet: Start with tasks that require a clean and dry mixing bowl (e.g. grinding sugar, chopping herbs).

Cold to hot: Whip cream, blend drinks, or chop onions before cooking sauces or soups.

All in one: For sauces, batters and cake mixes, you can add most ingredients at once and mix them in a few seconds. Also, whenever possible, cook several dishes at the same time using the simmering basket and/or Varoma.

CHOP vegetables before sautéing them. Chopping vegetables together with olive oil can make it easier or sometimes even unnecessary to scrape down the mixing bowl.

COOK WITH MILK OR CREAM at 90-95°C to avoid over-boiling. Stir sauces quickly to avoid lumps, on speed 2-4.

SAUTÉ onions or other chopped vegetables at 120°C for maximum flavour, between 3 and 7 minutes, depending on the ingredients' water content. Stir on speed 🥄 to 1.

COOK OR STEW at 90-100°C to retain as many nutrients as possible. Cooking time depends on ingredients, so refer to a similar Thermomix™ recipe for guidance.
Use 🔄 to stir or mix without chopping.

CRUSH ice together with drink ingredients to create refreshing cocktails or juices. A quick rinse is all that's needed to be ready for the next recipe.

BLEND soups, smoothies and sauces on speeds 6-10. Allow contents to cool a little before blending on high speeds and remember to increase speed gradually.

Continued on page 28 ▶

MIX sauces, cake batters, pancake batters or biscuit doughs in a few seconds on speeds 2-5. Note that all ingredients can usually be mixed all at once.

WHISKING egg whites requires a perfectly clean bowl, so start with this task whenever possible and remember to use the butterfly whisk.

COOK/STEAM IN THE SIMMERING BASKET OR VAROMA

ingredients such as vegetables, rice, whole shrimp, meatballs and many more. Add liquid to the mixing bowl, or cook them at the same time as you cook another dish in the mixing bowl.

GRIND grains, nuts or sugar, grate cheese or bread, as a first step. These tasks work best in a clean and dry mixing bowl, and little to no cleaning will be required before the next step.

KNEAD bread, pizza or pasta dough before other tasks. These doughs are usually easy to remove from the bowl, which avoids unnecessary cleaning.

white birthday cake

- 750 g cake flour, sifted
- 2 TB baking powder
- 180 g butter, softened
- 600 g sugar
- 500 ml milk
- 1 tsp vanilla extract
- 12 egg whites

Preheat oven to 160°C.

Sift together fl...

Steamed Vietnamese Fish
(with ginger, spring onions and soy)

- 675 g whole white fish (bass, plaice)

Sourdough Rye Bread

For the starter
- 330 g whole grain rye flour
- a pinch of instant yeast

For the dough
- 250 g rye flour
- 250 g whole wheat or white f...
- 1 TB salt
- 150 g cracked rye or rye fl...
- 560 ml water

TIPS ON TEMPERATURES

- **37°C**: Warm baby food and yeast (body temperature).
- **40-55°C**: Melt or warm gently (e.g. chocolate).
- **60-80°C**: Cook gently as in a bain-marie (this is ideal for sauces).
- **80-95°C**: Heat water for tea, heat milk without over-boiling.
- **100°C**: Boil water, cook soups and stews, preserving nutrients.
- **105-115°C**: Cook sugar syrup.
- **120°C**: Sauté onions or meat to extract flavour.
- **Varoma**: Steam ingredients while preserving their nutrients.

Please note that the actual cooking temperature of the food in the mixing bowl will rarely exceed 100°C, as this is the boiling point for water and most ingredients contain significant amounts of water.

TIPS ON SPEEDS

- **Speed** 🥄: Stir as if you were mixing with a wooden spoon, e.g. for risotto.
- **Speed 1-3**: Mix more or less gently, whip cream (speed 3), mash potatoes or chop soft ingredients (e.g. hard boiled eggs, raw mushrooms).
- **Speed 4-6**: Chop (e.g. onions, carrots), emulsify (e.g. mayonnaise, hollandaise sauce) or crush ice.
- **Speed 7-10** and **Turbo**: Grind or mill (e.g. sugar, wheat, coffee), blend to a completely smooth texture (e.g. creamy soups, smoothies, ice cream or sorbet) or chop hard ingredients (e.g. cured ham, hard cheeses).
- **Reverse (⟳) with low speeds (🥄 to 3)** will prevent delicate foods from falling apart.
- **Reverse (⟳) with higher speeds (4-10)** can be used for shredding ingredients without chopping them.
- Use **dough mode** for any dough that requires kneading (usually yeast doughs).

USEFUL CONVERSIONS

Certain traditional recipes rely on **volume measurements**. The following table provides useful conversion ratios for common ingredients:

1 tsp = 5 ml
1 tbsp = 3 tsp = 15 ml
1 US cup = 8 fluid ounces = 16 tbsp = 240 ml
1 tbsp water = 15 g/1 US cup water = 240 g
100 ml water = 10 cl = 100 g
1 tbsp flour = 8 g/1 US cup flour = 130 g

1 tbsp sugar = 12 g/1 US cup sugar = 200 g
1 tbsp icing sugar = 8 g/1 US cup icing sugar = 120 g
1 tbsp butter = 14 g/1 US cup butter = 230 g
1 tbsp oil = 14 g/1 US cup oil = 220 g
100 ml oil = 10 cl = 90 g
1 tsp salt = 6 g

Oven temperatures:
Celsius/Fahrenheit
150°C/300°F
160°C/320°F
170°C/340°F
180°C/355°F
190°C/375°F
200°C/390°F
210°C/410°F
220°C/430°F

BASICS

This chapter contains recipes that can be used in several other chapters of the cookbook, or as elements of recipes from other cookbooks. We will use these basic recipes as an opportunity to illustrate a few of the many functions of Thermomix™.

CHOPPING FUNCTIONS

Use this table as a guideline. You may adapt ingredient
amounts. In certain cases (e.g. chopping nuts), results
will be more consistent if you process the ingredient
in several batches instead of increasing the quantity.

FOOD	AMOUNT	TIME/SPEED	TIPS/VARIATIONS
GRATE			
Carrots	700 g, cut into pieces	**4-5 sec/speed 5**	
Cabbage (white/red)	400 g, cut into pieces	**10-12 sec/speed 4**	
Fruit (e.g. apples, pears)	600 g, cut into pieces	**4-5 sec/speed 4**	
Chocolate, coarse	200 g, cut into pieces	**4-5 sec/speed 7**	
Chocolate, fine	200 g, cut into pieces	**6-8 sec/speed 8**	
Bread, coarse	100 g bread, fresh or stale, cut into pieces (3 cm)	**9-10 sec/speed 4**	• Use any white or light crusty bread such as baguette, ciabatta, country bread, whole wheat bread or bread rolls. • You can add herbs or garlic to the bread before grating. • Breadcrumbs made from dry bread will keep for several weeks if stored in an air-tight container. • Breadcrumbs made from fresh bread must be stored in the freezer.
Bread roll, fine	100 g bread, fresh or stale, cut into pieces (3 cm)	**15-20 sec/speed 7**	
Potatoes	1000 g, cut into pieces	**12-15 sec/speed 5**	• Use peeled or unpeeled potatoes, as desired.
Cheese, medium-hard (e.g. Gruyère, Emmental)	200 g, cut into pieces	**10-12 sec/speed 5**	
Parmesan cheese (or other hard cheese)	100 g, cut into pieces (3 cm)	**15-20 sec/speed 10**	• Remove crusts

Continued on page 34 ▶

Grated carrots

Grated chocolate

Grated cheese

Grated Parmesan cheese

Breadcrumbs

▶ **CHOPPING FUNCTIONS,** continued

FOOD	AMOUNT	TIME	TIPS/VARIATIONS
CHOP/CRUSH/MINCE			
Herbs	20 g	**3 sec/speed 8**	• Patted dry with a paper towel
Garlic	1 clove	**2-4 sec/speed 8**	
Onion	50-200 g, cut into halves	**3-5 sec/speed 5**	
Ice cubes	200 g	**3-8 sec/speed 5**	• The length of time depends on size of ice cubes and how finely crushed you desire it. • The quantity of ice can be increased as long as ice cubes do not exceed the 1 litre mark in the mixing bowl.
Meat (e.g. beef, pork)	300 g, cut into pieces (3 cm), partially frozen	**10-12 sec/speed 6**	• You can use any kind of meat (e.g. beef, pork, lamb, poultry). • To achieve a uniform result, cut meat into evenly sized pieces. • The best consistency is often achieved with meat that is frozen for 60 minutes. However make sure it is only partially frozen.
Nuts (e.g. almonds, hazelnuts), coarse	200 g	**5-7 sec/speed 6**	
GRIND/MILL			
Nuts (e.g. almonds, hazelnuts), fine	200 g	**8-10 sec/speed 7**	
Cereal grains, fine (flour)	250 g cereal grains (e.g. wheat, rye, spelt, buckwheat, millet) or dried pulses (e.g. chickpeas, lentils, dried beans)	**1 min/speed 10**	• For best results, grind up to 250 g at a time. If more flour is needed, repeat the process in batches of up to 250 g.
Coffee beans	100-250 g	**1 min/speed 9**	
Poppy seeds	250 g	**30 sec/speed 9**	
Peppercorns, coarse	10 g	**10 sec-1 min/speed 10**	• Increase time for a finer grind.
Rice	100 g	**1-1 min 30 sec/speed 10**	
Sesame seeds, fine	200 g	**16-18 sec/speed 9**	
Spices	20 g	**1 min/speed 9**	
Sugar	200 g	**15-20 sec/speed 10**	• For best results, grind sugar in 100-200 g batches. • Icing sugar can be stored for long periods of time in an air-tight container.

Crushed ice

Chopped herbs

Chopped onions

Flour from cereal grains or pulses

Icing sugar

Minced meat

STEAMING FUNCTIONS

Use this table as a guideline, adjusting amounts and times according to your preference. Cooking times will vary depending on the quantity, quality, density and size of ingredients. If ingredients seem undercooked, simply extend the cooking time. To extend cooking time beyond 30 minutes, add 250 g water for each additional 15 minutes. Make sure a few holes in the Varoma dish and Varoma tray remain unobstructed, and that the Varoma lid is properly closed.

Place 500 g water or broth into the mixing bowl and steam **stated time/Varoma/speed 1**.

FOOD	AMOUNT	TIME	TIPS/VARIATIONS
VEGETABLES			
Carrots	800 g, cut into slices (0.5 cm)	**30 min**	
Carrots	800 g, whole, very thin	**25-30 min**	
Broccoli florets	800 g	**15 min**	
Cauliflower florets	800 g	**20-25 min**	
Cabbage	800 g, cut into strips	**23-25 min**	
Asparagus	800 g	**20-35 min**	Time varies according to diameter of stalks
Peppers	500 g, cut into strips (1 cm)	**15 min**	
Button mushrooms	500 g	**15 min**	
Peas, frozen	500 g	**16-18 min**	
Potatoes, new, small	500 g	**30 min**	
Potatoes	800 g, cut into medium-size pieces	**25-30 min**	
Leek	800 g, cut into slices	**25 min**	
Green beans	800 g, whole	**15-30 min**	
Fennel	800 g, cut into quarters	**30 min**	
Fennel	800 g, cut into slices	**18-20 min**	
Spinach, fresh	500 g	**10-12 min**	not more than 500 g
Courgettes	800 g, cut into slices (1 cm)	**25 min**	

FOOD	AMOUNT	TIME	TIPS/VARIATIONS

FRUIT

FOOD	AMOUNT	TIME	TIPS/VARIATIONS
Apples	500 g, cut into quarters	**12-15 min**	
Pears	800 g, cut into quarters	**12-15 min**	
Pears	800 g, cut into halves	**20 min**	
Apricots	500 g, cut into halves	**10-15 min**	
Peaches	500 g, cut into halves	**10-15 min**	
Plums	500 g, cut into halves	**12 min**	

FISH & SEAFOOD

FOOD	AMOUNT	TIME	TIPS/VARIATIONS
Fish fillets (2-2.5 cm thick)	800 g	**20 min**	e.g. salmon
Mussels, in the shell	500 g	**15 min**	
Prawns, raw, with shell	800 g	**10-15 min**	for frozen prawns, increase time by 2 min.
Trout	2 whole	**15 min**	

MEAT

FOOD	AMOUNT	TIME	TIPS/VARIATIONS
Meatballs	500 g	**25 min**	apricot-size
Chicken breasts	600 g	**20-25 min**	
Turkey escalopes	600 g	**20-25 min**	
Frankfurter sausages	6 pieces	**10-15 min**	depending on thickness

Broccoli

Pears

Fish fillets

VANILLA SUGAR

INGREDIENTS

1 vanilla pod, cut into pieces
200 g sugar

USEFUL ITEMS

1 jam jar with twist-off lid

PREPARATION

1. Place vanilla pod pieces and sugar into a jam jar with a twist-off lid. Close jar and shake to mix vanilla pod pieces with sugar. Allow to dry for 2-3 days.
2. Place jar contents into mixing bowl and grind **20 sec/speed 10**. Use vanilla sugar as needed or transfer back into jam jar and store in a dry place.

TIPS

• 1 tsp homemade vanilla sugar is roughly equivalent to 3 tsp (15 g) shop-bought vanilla sugar.
• Use vanilla pods left over from other recipes (rinse and dry pods after first use). This vanilla sugar will not be as strong and aromatic.

VARIATION

• **Quick version:** Without drying them first, place vanilla pod pieces with the sugar into the mixing bowl and grind **1 min/speed 10**. This vanilla sugar will be flavourful, but may have a tendency to clump.

 5 min   3 d   easy  1 total recipe (200 g)
1 total recipe:
Energy 3349 kJ/801 kcal
Protein 0 g/Carbs 200 g/Fat 0 g

WHIPPED CREAM

INGREDIENTS

200-600 g cream, min. 30% fat, chilled

Step 1

PREPARATION

1. **Insert butterfly whisk.** Place cream into mixing bowl and whip **speed 3**, without setting a time, until desired stiffness is achieved, watching carefully to avoid over-whipping. Use whipped cream as needed.

TIPS

- The required time depends on the temperature, fat content and quantity of cream.
- Take care not to over-whip or the cream will turn into butter. Watch carefully through the hole in the mixing bowl lid, and listen for a change in the mixing sound.
- The temperature of the cream before whipping should be 5-6°C, and the mixing bowl should be as cold as possible.
- The higher the fat content, the easier it is to whip the cream to a stiff texture.
- For best results, use 400-600 g cream.

VARIATION

- For sweetened whipped cream, before whipping add 1 tsp sugar, icing sugar or vanilla sugar per 200 g cream.

 10 min   10 min easy  1 total recipe (200-600 g)

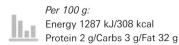 *Per 100 g:*
Energy 1287 kJ/308 kcal
Protein 2 g/Carbs 3 g/Fat 32 g

WHISKED EGG WHITES

INGREDIENTS

4 egg whites

Step 1

PREPARATION

1. **Insert butterfly whisk** into very clean mixing bowl (see tip). Place egg whites into mixing bowl and whisk **4 min/speed 3.5** or until stiff. Use whisked egg whites as needed.

TIPS

- The mixing bowl and butterfly whisk must be absolutely clean and free of any fatty residues.
- For best results, use whites from eggs that are approx. 7-14 days old.
- For a stiffer result, add a pinch of salt or a few tsp sugar half way through the whisking process.
- You can whisk between 2-8 egg whites at a time. Whisking time is approx. 1 minute per egg white.

 5 min

 5 min

 easy

 1 total recipe (approx. 150 g)

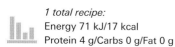
1 total recipe:
Energy 71 kJ/17 kcal
Protein 4 g/Carbs 0 g/Fat 0 g

SHORTCRUST PASTRY

INGREDIENTS

150 g flour
75 g butter, unsalted, cut into
        pieces
½ tsp salt
50 g water

USEFUL ITEMS

cling film

PREPARATION

1. Place flour, butter, salt and water into mixing bowl and mix
   20 sec/speed 4. Remove pastry from mixing bowl and form into
   a flattened ball. Wrap in cling film and refrigerate until needed,
   or use pastry as described in other recipes.

TIPS

• Use shortcrust pastry for sweet or savoury tarts.
• Unbaked shortcrust pastry freezes well. Freeze dough partially rolled out for faster
  defrosting in the refrigerator.
• To blind bake a tart case, use a rolling pin to roll out pastry on a lightly floured surface.
  Line a greased quiche or tart tin with the pastry and prick with a fork to avoid air
  bubbles. Line pastry with baking paper and fill with baking weights (e. g. rice, beans)
  before baking in a preheated oven (180°C) for 15 minutes. Remove baking paper and
  baking weights and bake for a further 5 minutes or until golden brown.

 5 min

 5 min
(baking not
included)

 easy

 1 total recipe
(1 large tart
Ø 26 cm)

1 total recipe:
Energy 4511 kJ/1078 kcal
Protein 16 g/Carbs 109 g/Fat 64 g

SWEET SHORTCRUST PASTRY

INGREDIENTS

100 g sugar
200 g butter, unsalted, cut into
      pieces
370 g flour
1 egg
1 pinch salt
1½ tsp vanilla sugar, homemade
      or 1 tsp natural vanilla extract

USEFUL ITEMS

cling film
tart tin (Ø 26-28 cm) or baking tray
      and paper
rolling pin
biscuit cutters
cooling rack

PREPARATION

1. Place sugar into mixing bowl and grind **15 sec/speed 10**.
2. Add butter, flour, egg, salt and vanilla sugar into mixing bowl and mix **25-30 sec/speed 5** with aid of spatula. Remove pastry dough from mixing bowl, form into a flattened ball and wrap with cling film. Refrigerate for 1 hour.
3. Preheat oven to 180°C. Grease a tart tin or line a baking tray with baking paper and set aside.
4. Roll out dough between 2 sheets of baking paper or cling film to a thickness of 5 mm. Line prepared tart tin with dough or cut out shapes and place them on prepared baking tray. For a tart case, prick pastry with fork to avoid air bubbles. Bake tart case for 15-20 minutes (180°C), biscuits for 10-12 minutes (180°C), or until golden. Allow to cool completely on a cooling rack before decorating, filling, or storing in an air-tight container.

TIPS

- Be careful not to knead the dough unnecessarily with your hands, as this will make the biscuits or tart case tough.
- If the dough becomes warm and difficult to work with, place rolled out dough, still covered with sheets of baking paper or cling film, into refrigerator until dough is firm enough to handle.
- Instead of rolling out the dough with a rolling pin, shape it into a log. For biscuits, roll the log so the cross section is round. For a tart case, make a flatter log. Wrap log in cling film and refrigerate until firm enough to cut into slices. For biscuits, cut round log into round slices (5 mm thick) and bake as directed by the recipe. For a tart case, line the tart tin with long dough slices (5 mm thick), overlapping them slightly, and press dough with fingers to fill in any cracks. Bake as directed by the recipe.

VARIATIONS

- **Decorated biscuits:** decorate biscuit shapes with coloured icing, chocolate coating and sweets.
- **Jam-filled biscuits:** spread cool biscuit with jam and place another on top. Dust with icing sugar.

 20 min　　 1 h 50 min　　easy　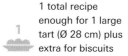 1 total recipe enough for 1 large tart (Ø 28 cm) plus extra for biscuits　 *1 total recipe:* Energy 13710 kJ/3277 kcal Protein 45 g/Carbs 376 g/Fat 175 g

Step 4

Tip

Variations

QUICK PUFF PASTRY

INGREDIENTS

200 g butter, unsalted, cut into
    small pieces (1-2 cm), frozen
200 g plain flour, plus extra for
    dusting
90 g water, chilled
½ tsp salt

USEFUL ITEMS

cling film
rolling pin
baking tray and paper
cooling rack

PREPARATION

1. Place butter, plain flour, chilled water and salt into mixing bowl and **mix 20 sec/speed 6**. Remove pastry dough from mixing bowl, form into a ball and flatten into a rough square. Wrap pastry square in cling film and refrigerate for 20 minutes.

2. Unwrap dough and place onto a lightly floured work surface. Using a rolling pin, roll out dough into a long rectangle 3 times as long as it is wide (approx. 60 cm x 20 cm). Fold dough into thirds and give folded dough a quarter turn so that the fold is on the left. Repeat rolling and folding process twice, then return to refrigerator for 20 minutes or place in freezer for 5 minutes before using.

3. Preheat oven to 200°C. Line a baking tray with baking paper and set aside.

4. Roll dough into a rectangle (5 mm thick) and cut into required shape or shapes right before baking. Bake for 20 minutes (200°C) for one large piece of pastry, 12-15 minutes (200°C) for smaller pastries, or as directed by other recipes. Allow to cool on a cooling rack before serving or storing in an air-tight container.

TIPS

• This pastry serves as a base for cakes, pastries, cream puffs and fruit tarts.
• The success of this recipe depends on keeping the pastry dough chilled so the layers of butter do not melt. A cold work surface (marble or stone) and a cool room temperature are helpful. If at any time during the process the dough feels warm, place into the freezer for 5 minutes before rolling out again. To prevent the dough from sticking to the work surface, whenever necessary use a light dusting of flour, or roll dough between two sheets of baking paper.
• Puff pastry dough freezes very well before baking. Defrost in the refrigerator before using. Partially rolling out the dough before freezing allows for faster defrosting.
• Once baked, pastry keeps well for up to 15 days stored in a sealed container in a cool dry place.

VARIATION

• Replace water with very cold white wine.

 20 min   1 h 20 min   medium    1 total recipe (490 g)    *1 total recipe:* Energy 9300 kJ/2223 kcal Protein 22 g/Carbs 152 g/Fat 168 g

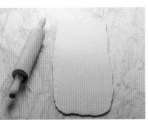

Step 2

CHOUX PASTRY

INGREDIENTS

150 g water
80 g butter, unsalted, cut into
    pieces
1 pinch salt
2 tsp sugar (10 g)
120 g flour
3 eggs (53-63 g each)

USEFUL ITEMS

baking tray and paper
icing bag and Ø 10 mm nozzle

PREPARATION

1. Place water, butter, salt and sugar into mixing bowl and bring to a boil **5 min/100°C/speed 1**.
2. Add flour and mix **20 sec/speed 4**. Remove mixing bowl and set aside to cool for 10 minutes.
3. Preheat oven to 200°C. Line a baking tray with baking paper and set aside.
4. Place mixing bowl back into position and mix **speed 5**, adding eggs one at a time through hole in mixing bowl lid onto rotating blades.
5. After adding the last egg, mix a further **30 sec/speed 5**.
6. Transfer pastry mixture into an icing bag and pipe balls (choux) or sticks (éclairs) onto prepared baking tray, leaving 5 cm space between each. Bake for 20-25 minutes (200°C) or until golden brown. Turn off oven and open oven door slightly, leaving it ajar for 10 minutes to allow choux pastries to dry. Remove tray from oven and allow choux pastries to cool completely before serving or filling as desired.

TIPS

- Use a wet finger to smooth down any bumps on the top of choux pastries before baking.
- If you don't have an icing bag, cut the corner off a sturdy freezer bag and use to pipe choux pastries onto baking tray.

VARIATIONS

- Choux pastries can be filled with whipped cream or pastry cream and served with fresh fruit, dusted with sugar.
- Fill choux pastries with cream cheese and fresh herbs for a savoury option.
- Adjust the size and shape of the choux pastries to suit your taste and requirements.

 20 min   2 h   medium   **18** 18 pieces    *Per piece:* Energy 300 kJ/72 kcal Protein 2 g/Carbs 6 g/Fat 5 g

Step 2

Step 5

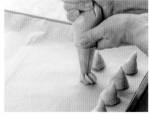

Step 6

Tip

CRÊPES

INGREDIENTS

50 g butter, unsalted,
     plus extra for frying
500 g milk
200 g water
250 g flour
4 eggs
1 pinch salt

USEFUL ITEMS

non-stick pan (Ø 22 cm)
turner
kitchen towel

PREPARATION

1. Place butter into mixing bowl and melt **2 min/70°C/speed 2**.
2. Add milk, water, flour, eggs and salt into mixing bowl and mix **20 sec/speed 4**. The batter should have the consistency of liquid cream. If it seems too thick, add a little milk. Allow batter to rest for at least 30 minutes before using.
3. Lightly grease a non-stick frying pan with butter and heat on medium-high. Pour in a small ladle of batter, twirling the pan as you pour to cover base of pan completely. Cook for 2-3 minutes or until edges of crêpe are light golden. Turn crêpe over and cook for a further 1 minute. Transfer to a plate and cover with a kitchen towel to keep warm. Repeat with remaining batter. Serve warm.

TIPS
• Crêpes can be served with sweet or savoury fillings.
• Crêpes can be frozen for later use. Place a piece of baking paper or cling film between each crêpe before freezing so they can be easily defrosted. After defrosting, wrap crêpes in aluminium foil and warm in a preheated oven (150°C) for 5-10 minutes.

VARIATIONS
• To replace butter with oil, omit step 1 and add 50 g oil along with all other ingredients in step 2. Use oil instead of butter for frying.
• Flavour the crêpes in step 2: add 40 g vanilla sugar, 1 tsp grated orange zest, or 80 g sugar and 2 tbsp rum.

Step 3

 45 min   1 h 15 min   easy   10 pieces

Per piece:
Energy 872 kJ/209 kcal
Protein 7 g/Carbs 21 g/Fat 11 g

AMERICAN-STYLE PANCAKES

INGREDIENTS

50 g butter, unsalted,
    plus extra for frying
300 g milk
2 eggs
30 g sugar
200 g plain flour
1 tbsp baking powder (15 g)
½ tsp salt

USEFUL ITEMS

frying pan
turner

PREPARATION

1. Place butter into mixing bowl and melt **2 min/70°C/speed 1**.
2. Add milk, eggs, sugar, plain flour, baking powder and salt and mix **10 sec/speed 5**.
3. To cook pancakes, heat ½ tsp butter in a frying pan over medium heat. For each pancake, pour in a ladle of batter and cook 1-2 minutes or until bubbles start bursting on pancake surface. Turn pancake over and cook for a further 1 minute. Place pancake onto a serving plate and cover to keep warm. Repeat with remaining batter. Serve hot.

TIPS

• Serve pancakes with maple syrup, whipped cream, chocolate, caramel sauce or jam.

VARIATIONS

• To replace butter with oil, omit step 1 and add 50 g oil along with all other ingredients in step 2. Use oil instead of butter for frying.
• **Blueberry or raspberry pancakes:** scatter 1 tbsp berries onto each pancake right after pouring batter into pan, before bubbles start to form.
• **Chocolate pancakes:** add 2 tsp cocoa powder in step 2.

Step 3

 40 min   40 min    easy   12   12 pieces (Ø 12-14 cm)    *Per piece:* Energy 548 kJ/131 kcal Protein 4 g/Carbs 16 g/Fat 6 g

PIZZA DOUGH

INGREDIENTS

30 g extra virgin olive oil, plus extra
  for greasing
220 g water, room temperature
1 tsp sugar or malt powder
  (optional)
20 g fresh yeast, crumbled or
  2 tsp dried instant yeast (8 g)
400 g bread flour
1 tsp salt

USEFUL ITEMS

cling film

PREPARATION

1. Lightly grease a large bowl and set aside. Place water, sugar and fresh yeast into mixing bowl and mix **20 sec/speed 2**.
2. Add bread flour, extra virgin olive oil and salt and knead **2 min/⚘**. Place dough into prepared bowl and form into a ball. Cover bowl with cling film and let dough rise until doubled in size (approx. 1 hour). Use pizza dough as needed.

TIPS

• In step 2, the cling film can be lightly oiled to prevent it from sticking to the rising dough.
• Use dough to make 1 large rectangular pizza or 4 individual round pizzas.
• To shape pizza, place dough on a baking tray (approx. 40 x 35 cm) lined with baking paper or greased with extra virgin olive oil. Press it out with your finger tips from the centre to the edges, and gently stretch it into shape. Alternatively you can roll it out with a rolling pin on a floured surface and transfer it to a baking tray lined with baking paper.
• To bake pizza, form a small ridge around the edge, and spread lightly with desired topping. Bake for 20-25 minutes in a preheated oven (230°C).

 5 min

 1 h
(baking not
included)

 easy

1
1 total recipe
(670 g)

1 total recipe:
Energy 7341 kJ/1752 kcal
Protein 45 g/Carbs 302 g/Fat 39 g

FRESH PASTA DOUGH

INGREDIENTS

200 g plain flour, plus extra for dusting
2 eggs (53-63 g each)
1 tbsp extra virgin olive oil
water
salt

USEFUL ITEMS

cling film
rolling pin or pasta machine
large saucepan

PREPARATION

1. Place plain flour, eggs and extra virgin olive oil into mixing bowl and knead **2 min/**. Dough will appear crumbly. Pat dough into a ball, wrap in cling film and allow to rest for 15 minutes.
2. Roll out dough on a floured surface into thin (2-3 mm) rectangular shapes, either with a rolling pin or with a pasta machine. Dust pasta lightly with flour to prevent it from sticking. Cut pasta into desired shapes according to the type of pasta you are making:
   Lasagne or ravioli: Cut dough into sheets (approx. 20 cm x 10 cm).
   Tagliatelle: Cut into strips (2 cm x max. 30 cm).
   Farfalle: Cut into small rectangular shapes (2 cm x 5 cm) and pinch centre of each rectangle to form a butterfly shape.
3. Cook pasta in a large quantity of salted boiling water (approx. 1 tsp salt per litre of water) for 3-4 minutes, depending on shape and thickness of pasta. Serve hot, with sauce as desired.

TIPS

- Serve pasta as a side or main dish with tomato sauce, pesto or your favourite sauce.
- Roll out small amounts of dough at a time and cover remaining dough with a damp kitchen towel to prevent it from drying out.
- For best results, after rolling and cutting allow pasta to dry 1-2 hours on a floured cloth.
- To increase quantity, add 1 extra egg per added 100 g flour. The maximum quantity at any one time is 500 g flour and 5 eggs. Increase kneading time to 3 minutes.

VARIATIONS

- **Green pasta dough:** use basic recipe with an added 100 g flour and 70 g spinach leaves (fresh, clean and dry; or frozen, defrosted and water squeezed out). Place 300 g flour and spinach leaves into mixing bowl and mix **20 sec/speed 9**. Add eggs and oil and knead **2 min/**.
- **Red pasta dough without eggs:** instead of 2 eggs, use 100 g tomato juice and proceed as directed by the recipe.

 40 min   1 h   advanced 4 4 portions

Per portion:
Energy 1049 kJ/251 kcal
Protein 9 g/Carbs 39 g/Fat 6 g

Step 1

Step 2

BOILED EGGS

INGREDIENTS

400 g water, room temperature
4 eggs (53-63 g each), chilled

PREPARATION

1. Place water into mixing bowl, insert simmering basket and place eggs into it. Steam **time according to taste/Varoma/speed 1**.
   Cooking time depends on how you like your eggs:
   10 minutes very runny (egg yolk liquid, egg white viscous)
   11 minutes runny (egg yolk liquid, egg white firm)
   12 minutes soft (egg yolk soft)
   13 minutes firm boiled
   14 minutes hard boiled
2. Immediately remove simmering basket with spatula and place it with eggs under cold running water to stop cooking. Use boiled eggs as needed.

TIP
• Using eggs at room temperature, smaller eggs or hot water will shorten cooking time.

 5 min   20 min   easy   4 pieces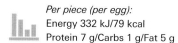

Per piece (per egg):
Energy 332 kJ/79 kcal
Protein 7 g/Carbs 1 g/Fat 5 g

BOILED PASTA

INGREDIENTS

1200 g water
1½ tsp salt
320 g dried pasta, short or long
(e.g. penne, spaghetti)

PREPARATION

1. Place water into mixing bowl and bring to a boil
10 min/100°C/speed 1.
2. Add salt and dried pasta through hole in mixing bowl lid and
cook without measuring cup for **time indicated on packet/
100°C/⟳/speed 1**, or until al dente. Drain pasta through Varoma
dish and serve hot, plain or with a sauce as desired.

TIPS
• The maximum quantity of pasta that can be cooked at any one time is 500 g.
When cooking 500 g pasta, increase the quantity of water to 1500 g and boiling
time in step 1 to 14 minutes.
• Long pasta such as spaghetti will initially stick out of the hole in the mixing bowl lid,
then drop into the mixing bowl as it softens. If necessary, cook a further 2 minutes.
• If water bubbles up into the mixing bowl lid while pasta is cooking, add 1 tsp oil or
butter to the cooking water to reduce frothing.

Step 2

 5 min   20 min   easy   4 portions

Per portion:
Energy 1164 kJ/278 kcal
Protein 10 g/Carbs 56 g/Fat 1 g

STEAMED RICE

INGREDIENTS

1000 g water
1½ tsp salt
20 g olive oil or butter (optional)
50-350 g long-grain white rice

PREPARATION

1. Place water, salt and olive oil into mixing bowl. Insert simmering basket, weigh rice into it and cook **20 min/100°C/speed 4**. Transfer rice into a serving dish and serve hot.

TIP
- Certain types of rice require rinsing (check packet instructions). Place simmering basket into empty mixing bowl, weigh rice into it, remove simmering basket and rinse rice thoroughly under running water. Proceed as directed by the recipe.

VARIATION
- For other types of rice, adjust the cooking time according to the time indicated on rice packet. For example:
Short-grain rice: 18 minutes
Basmati rice: 15 minutes
Parboiled rice: 20-22 minutes

 5 min   25 min   easy    1-6 portions (50-350 g rice)    *Per portion:* Energy 857 kJ/205 kcal Protein 4 g/Carbs 45 g/Fat 0 g

VEGETABLE STOCK PASTE

INGREDIENTS

50 g Parmesan cheese,
      cut into pieces (3 cm) (optional)
200 g celery stalks, cut into pieces
250 g carrots, cut into pieces
100 g onions, cut into halves
100 g tomatoes, cut into pieces
150 g courgettes, cut into pieces
1 garlic clove
50 g fresh mushrooms
1 dried bay leaf (optional)
6 sprigs mixed fresh herbs
      (e.g. basil, sage, rosemary),
      leaves only
4 sprigs fresh parsley
120 g coarse salt
30 g dry white wine
1 tbsp olive oil

USEFUL ITEMS

air-tight jar

PREPARATION

1. Place Parmesan cheese into mixing bowl and grate **10 sec/speed 10**. Transfer into a bowl and set aside.
2. Place celery stalks, carrots, onions, tomatoes, courgettes, garlic clove, fresh mushrooms, dried bay leaf, mixed fresh herbs and parsley into mixing bowl and chop **10 sec/speed 7** with aid of spatula. Scrape down sides of mixing bowl with spatula.
3. Add coarse salt, dry white wine and olive oil.
   Cook **35 min/Varoma/speed 2**, placing simmering basket instead of measuring cup onto mixing bowl lid to help prevent splashing. Mixture will become thick and fairly dry.
4. Remove simmering basket, add reserved Parmesan cheese, insert measuring cup and blend **20 sec/speed 10**. Transfer into an air-tight jar and allow to cool before using or storing in refrigerator.

TIPS
- 1 heaped tsp stock paste is roughly equivalent to 1 shop-bought vegetable stock cube for 0.5 l.
- To make vegetable stock, use 1 heaped tsp per 500 g water.
- Stock paste keeps in the refrigerator for several months.
- The salt in this recipe is used as the preserving agent. When mixed with water as described above, the stock does not taste too salty.
- If you wish to decrease the salt in the recipe, you must store the stock paste in the freezer.

VARIATIONS
- Adapt the stock paste recipe using the natural ingredients of your choice.
- Add more mushrooms for a vegetable stock paste with a stronger mushroom flavour.

 20 min   50 min   easy   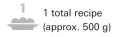 1 total recipe (approx. 500 g)   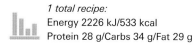 *1 total recipe:* Energy 2226 kJ/533 kcal Protein 28 g/Carbs 34 g/Fat 29 g

MEAT STOCK PASTE

INGREDIENTS

300 g meat pieces, sinew free,
    cut into pieces
300 g mixed vegetables
    (e.g. celery stalk, carrots,
    onions, garlic, tomatoes),
    cut into pieces
4 sprigs mixed fresh herbs
    (e.g. sage, rosemary),
    leaves only
150 g coarse salt
30 g red wine
1 dried bay leaf
1 whole clove

USEFUL ITEMS

air-tight jar

PREPARATION

1. Place meat pieces into mixing bowl and mince **10 sec/speed 7**. Transfer into a bowl and set aside.
2. Place mixed vegetables and mixed fresh herbs into mixing bowl and chop **10 sec/speed 5**. Scrape down sides of mixing bowl with spatula.
3. Add coarse salt, red wine, bay leaf, whole clove and reserved minced meat. Cook **25 min/Varoma/speed 2**, placing simmering basket instead of measuring cup onto mixing bowl lid to help prevent splashing. Mixture will thicken and become fairly dry.
4. Remove simmering basket, insert measuring cup and blend **1 min/speed 7**. Transfer into an air-tight jar and allow to cool before using or storing in refrigerator.

TIPS
- 1 heaped tsp stock paste is roughly equivalent to 1 shop-bought meat stock cube for 0.5 l.
- To make meat stock, use 1 heaped tsp per 500 g water.
- Stock paste keeps in the refrigerator for several months.
- The salt in this recipe is used as the preserving agent. When mixed with water as described above, the stock does not taste too salty.
- If you wish to decrease the salt in the recipe, you must store the stock paste in the freezer.

VARIATION
- Adapt the stock paste recipe using the natural ingredients of your choice.

 20 min   45 min   easy    1 total recipe (approx. 400 g)   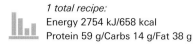 *1 total recipe:* Energy 2754 kJ/658 kcal Protein 59 g/Carbs 14 g/Fat 38 g

CHICKEN STOCK PASTE

INGREDIENTS

300 g chicken meat, skinless,
  boneless and sinew free (from
  approx. 500 g chicken legs),
  cut into pieces
200 g mixed white vegetables
  (e.g. celeriac, onions, garlic,
  leek), cut into pieces as needed
4 sprigs mixed fresh herbs
  (e.g. rosemary, thyme, parsley),
  leaves only
150 g coarse salt
100 g white wine
1 dried bay leaf
1 whole clove
5 coriander seeds

USEFUL ITEMS

air-tight jar

PREPARATION

1. Place chicken meat into mixing bowl and mince **5 sec/speed 7**.
   Transfer into a bowl and set aside.
2. Place mixed white vegetables and mixed fresh herbs into mixing bowl
   and chop **10 sec/speed 5**. Scrape down sides of mixing bowl with
   spatula.
3. Add coarse salt, white wine, bay leaf, whole clove, coriander seeds
   and reserved minced chicken. Cook **25 min/Varoma/speed 2**,
   placing simmering basket instead of measuring cup onto mixing bowl
   lid to help prevent splashing. Mixture will thicken and become fairly dry.
4. Remove simmering basket, insert measuring cup and blend
   1 min/speed 7. Transfer into an air-tight jar and allow to cool
   before using or storing in refrigerator.

TIPS

- 1 heaped tsp stock paste is roughly equivalent to 1 shop-bought chicken stock cube
  for 0.5 l.
- To make chicken stock, use 1 heaped tsp per 500 g water.
- Stock paste keeps in the refrigerator for several months.
- The salt in this recipe is used as the preserving agent. When mixed with water
  as described above, the stock does not taste too salty.
- If you wish to decrease the salt in the recipe, you must store the stock paste in the
  freezer.

VARIATION

- Adapt the stock paste recipe using the natural ingredients of your choice.

 20 min 45 min easy  1 total recipe (approx. 400 g) 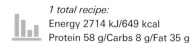 *1 total recipe:* Energy 2714 kJ/649 kcal Protein 58 g/Carbs 8 g/Fat 35 g

SUGAR ICING

INGREDIENTS

200 g sugar
1 egg white (35 g)
4-5 drops lemon juice

USEFUL ITEMS

pastry spatula

PREPARATION

1. Place sugar into mixing bowl and grind **20 sec/speed 10**.
2. Add egg white and lemon juice and mix **10 sec/speed 6**.
   Use sugar icing as needed.

TIPS

- Use to decorate cakes, pies, pastries, etc.
- Pour mixture over cake or pastry and spread with a heated pastry spatula, dipped in hot water and dried before use. Allow to rest until icing is set, approx. 2 hours.
- If icing is too thick, add a few more drops of lemon juice or water.
- For different colours, distribute icing in several bowls, add colouring to each bowl and combine.
- To decorate biscuits, outline a border using an icing bag with a thin nozzle and fill in shape with coloured icing.

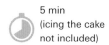 5 min

 5 min
(icing the cake
not included)

 easy

1
1 total recipe
(240 g)

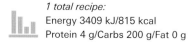
1 total recipe:
Energy 3409 kJ/815 kcal
Protein 4 g/Carbs 200 g/Fat 0 g

CHOCOLATE ICING (SIMPLE GANACHE)

INGREDIENTS

100 g dark chocolate,
   cut into pieces
80 g cream, min. 30% fat

PREPARATION

1. Place dark chocolate into mixing bowl and grate **10 sec/speed 8**. Scrape down sides of mixing bowl with spatula.
2. Add cream and melt **2 min/50°C/speed 3**. Allow ganache to cool slightly and thicken. Use chocolate icing (ganache) as needed.

TIPS

- Cover a cake with ganache, and allow to set before serving.
- Serve warm as a sauce over ice cream.
- Use ganache as a filling for biscuits or petits fours.

VARIATIONS

- Ganache can be whipped into a paler, fluffier icing. Once ganache has cooled completely, **insert butterfly whisk** and whip **1-2 min/speed 3**.
- **Chocolate truffles:** freeze ganache, allow to thaw slightly, take 2 tsp of ganache and roll into a small ball. Coat ball in unsweetened cocoa powder and repeat with remaining ganache. Store truffles in the refrigerator.

Variation

 5 min   20 min    easy   1 total recipe (180 g)

1 total recipe:
Energy 3107 kJ/742 kcal
Protein 10 g/Carbs 49 g/Fat 56 g

BUTTER ICING

INGREDIENTS

120 g caster sugar

350 g butter, unsalted, softened,
  cut into pieces

120 g milk

1 tsp natural vanilla extract
  (optional)

PREPARATION

1. Place sugar into mixing bowl and grind **20 sec/speed 10**.
2. **Insert butterfly whisk.** Add butter, milk and natural vanilla extract and mix **3 min/speed 3**. Use buttercream icing as needed.

TIPS

- Fill or ice cakes using a pastry spatula, or place icing in an icing bag to pipe decorations onto cakes or pastries.
- Buttercream icing can be kept in an air-tight container in the refrigerator for later use. Allow icing to soften at room temperature before using.

VARIATION

- The buttercream icing can be flavoured to taste. For example, in step 2, instead of vanilla extract add ½-1½ tsp instant coffee or 1-3 tsp cocoa powder or 2 tbsp praline (ground caramelised almonds) or any other flavouring.

Tip

 5 min   5 min   easy   1 total recipe (approx. 600 g)   *1 total recipe:* Energy 13323 kJ/3187 kcal Protein 6 g/Carbs 125 g/Fat 295 g

PLAIN YOGHURT

INGREDIENTS
1000 g whole milk,
120 g plain yoghurt, min. 1.8% fat
50 g milk powder (optional)

USEFUL ITEMS
8 air-tight jars or containers
blanket

PREPARATION

1. Place whole milk, plain yoghurt and milk powder into mixing bowl and warm **6 min/50°C/speed 3**. Transfer yoghurt mixture into 8 air-tight jars or small containers and wrap immediately in a blanket to keep warm. Leave jars well wrapped for 11-13 hours in a warm place (see tip) without moving them during this incubation period. Chill in refrigerator for at least 3 hours before serving.

TIPS
- Keeping the yoghurt warm and and undisturbed during incubation is essential to achieving the right texture. To increase insulation you can place wrapped jars in a picnic cooler or in a cool, turned-off oven.
- The cooler the room temperature, the longer the yoghurt should be left to incubate. In very warm environments, 8-10 hours may be sufficient.
- The longer the incubation time, the more acidic the yoghurt.
- For best results, make sure all utensils are very clean before making yoghurt.
- Avoid using low-fat milk or low-fat yoghurt for this recipe.
- Milk powder helps the yoghurt to set.
- If using raw milk, heat milk **10 min/90°C/speed 2**, then allow the milk to cool to room temperature before starting the recipe.
- The heating and cooling process described for raw milk can also be used with pasteurised milk to produce a thicker consistency.
- Remember to reserve some plain yoghurt as a starting culture for the next batch.

VARIATIONS
- For sweetened yoghurt, add 40 g sugar along with the other ingredients.
- For creamy yoghurt, add 100 g cream along with the other ingredients.

 10 min   14 h  easy 8 jars (each 140 g)  *Per jar:* Energy 371 kJ/89 kcal Protein 5 g/Carbs 7 g/Fat 5 g

STARTERS AND SALADS

CHOPPED VEGETABLE SALAD

INGREDIENTS

500 g mixed vegetables and fruit
    (e.g. 50 g celeriac,
    100 g beetroot,
    250 g carrots,
    100 g apple), cut into
    pieces as needed
20 g oil
20 g vinegar or lemon juice
1 tsp salt or herb salt
2 pinches ground black pepper
½ tsp sugar or honey

PREPARATION

1. Place mixed vegetables and fruit, oil, vinegar, salt, black pepper and sugar into mixing bowl. Chop **5 sec/speed 5** with aid of spatula and serve.

TIPS

- Chopping time depends on the consistency of the vegetables and fruit you have chosen (soft vegetables need a shorter chopping time). If you prefer a chunkier salad, chop at **speed 4.5**.
- Prepare your own herb salt with the Thermomix™.
- Serve on endive leaves or a bed of lettuce, or combine with lettuce leaves.

VARIATIONS

- Choose your preferred oil (e.g. extra virgin olive oil, nut oils, grape seed oil) and vinegar (e.g. balsamic vinegar, cider vinegar or fruit flavoured vinegars).
- Create your own salads using vegetables and/or fruit that you have at home or that are in season (e.g. cabbage, turnips, carrots, cauliflower, broccoli, peppers, courgettes, apples, pears, peaches).
- Mixing different vegetables or adding fruit is not required. You can make this salad with a single vegetable. For example use this recipe to make **carrot salad**.
- For added flavour and texture, add fresh herbs, 50 g nuts (e.g. hazelnuts, walnuts, almonds, cashews) or 20 g seeds (e.g. sunflower, pumpkin).

 10 min   10 min   easy   4 portions   

Per portion:
Energy 410 kJ/98 kcal
Protein 1 g/Carbs 11 g/Fat 5 g

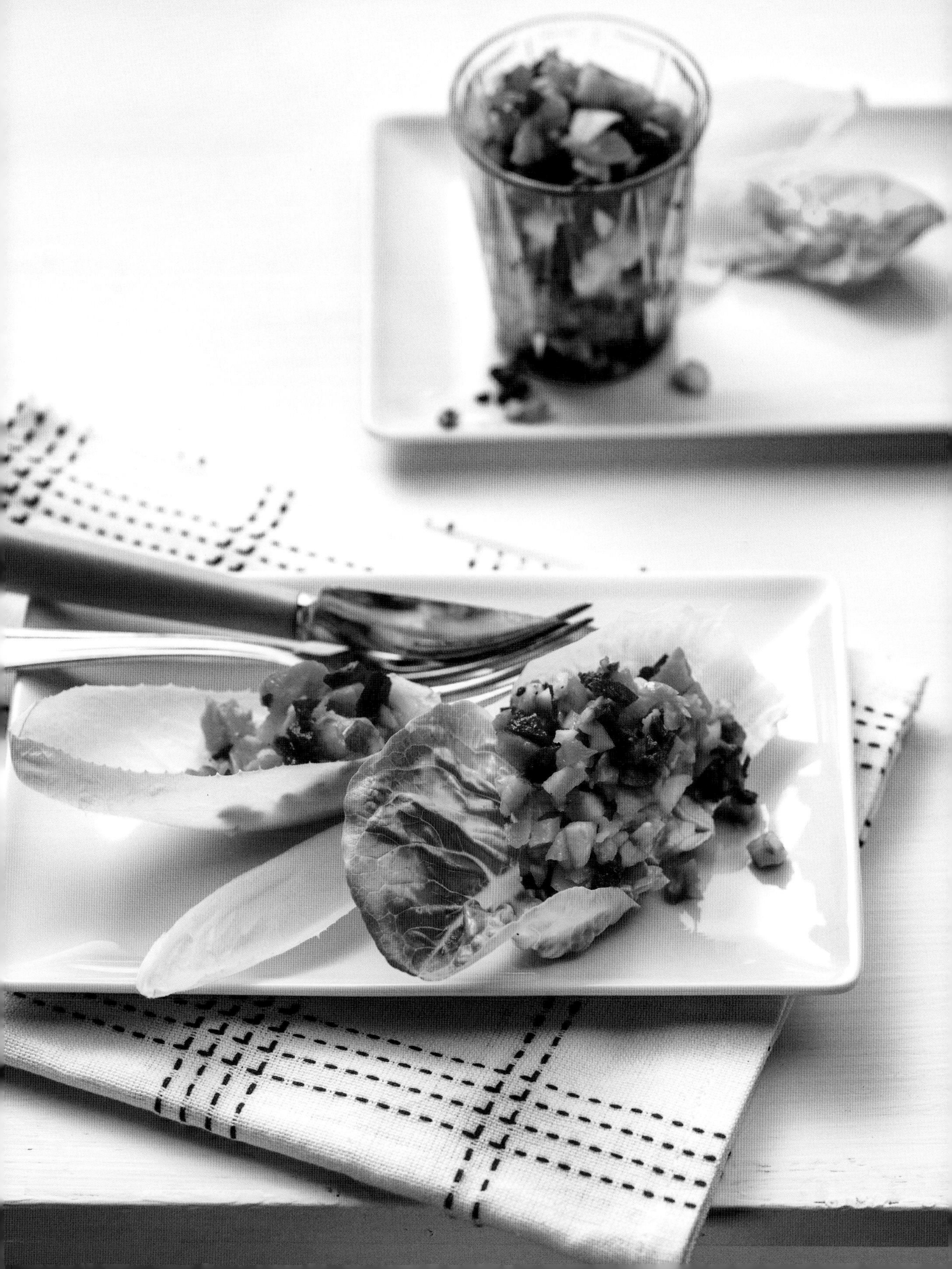

BROCCOLI SALAD WITH RED PEPPERS AND PINE NUTS

INGREDIENTS

300 g broccoli, cut into florets

1 red pepper (approx. 150 g),
     cut into pieces

1 apple (approx. 100 g),
     cut into quarters

30 g pine nuts or sunflower seeds

25 g olive oil

15 g fruit vinegar or white balsamic
     vinegar

1 tsp honey

1½ tsp mustard

1 tsp salt or herb salt

½ tsp ground black pepper

PREPARATION

1. Place broccoli, red pepper, apple, pine nuts, olive oil, fruit vinegar, honey, mustard, salt and black pepper into mixing bowl and chop **5 sec/speed 4**. Serve at room temperature.

VARIATION

• Pine nuts can also be replaced with other nuts.

 10 min   10 min   easy   6 / 6 portions   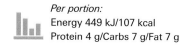 *Per portion:* Energy 449 kJ/107 kcal Protein 4 g/Carbs 7 g/Fat 7 g

BEETROOT SALAD

INGREDIENTS

400 g raw beetroot, peeled,
cut into quarters

100 g carrots, cut into pieces

20 g onions

1 green apple (approx. 100 g),
cut into quarters

2-3 sprigs fresh coriander, leaves
only, to taste, or fresh parsley,
leaves only, to taste

2 tbsp extra virgin olive oil

10-20 g lemon juice

¼ tsp salt, adjust to taste

1 pinch ground black pepper,
adjust to taste (optional)

1 pinch sugar, adjust to taste
(optional)

PREPARATION

1. Place beetroot, carrots, onions, apple, coriander, extra virgin olive oil, lemon juice, salt, black pepper and sugar into mixing bowl, chop **5-7 sec/speed 5** and serve.

VARIATIONS

- Serve beetroot salad on a bed of spinach leaves with crumbled goat cheese or feta cheese and pumpkin seeds or pistachio nuts.
- For extra flavour and sweetness, add 1 tsp pomegranate molasses or honey before chopping in step 1.

 10 min 10 min easy 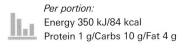 6 portions

Per portion:
Energy 350 kJ/84 kcal
Protein 1 g/Carbs 10 g/Fat 4 g

COLESLAW

INGREDIENTS

200 g cabbage, cut into pieces
100 g carrots, cut into pieces
1 green apple (approx. 100 g),
    cut into quarters
20 g onions, adjust to taste
    (optional)
1 pinch salt, adjust to taste
1 pinch ground black pepper,
    adjust to taste
2 tbsp mayonnaise, adjust to taste

PREPARATION

1. Place cabbage, carrots, green apple, onions, salt, ground black pepper and mayonnaise into mixing bowl, chop **4-6 sec/speed 5** and serve.

TIP
• Serve coleslaw at a barbecue or as a side dish with fish and chips, pork cutlets or chicken.

 10 min 10 min easy 4 portions

 *Per portion:*
Energy 554 kJ/133 kcal
Protein 1 g/Carbs 8 g/Fat 11 g

SALMON TARTARE

INGREDIENTS

1 tsp pink peppercorns,
  plus extra to garnish
2 sprigs fresh dill, leaves only,
  plus extra to garnish
300 g fresh salmon fillets
  (sushi quality), skinless,
  cut into 3 pieces
40 g lemon juice, freshly squeezed
2 tbsp olive oil
½ tsp Worcestershire sauce
½ tsp salt
1 pinch ground black pepper
100 g watercress leaves or mixed
  salad

PREPARATION

1. Place pink peppercorns and dill into mixing bowl and grind
   5 sec/speed 6. Scrape down sides of mixing bowl with spatula.
2. Add salmon fillets, lemon juice, olive oil, Worcestershire sauce,
   salt and ground black pepper and chop **4 sec/⟳/speed 5**.
3. Place watercress leaves onto 6 plates, top with salmon tartare and
   garnish with pink peppercorns and dill. Serve cold.

TIPS
• Only use very fresh high quality fish that is suitable for raw consumption.
• Serve with salted whipped cream.

VARIATION
• Instead of salmon use a fresh white fish or a mix of different fish, e.g. half salmon
  and half gilthead (bream) or half fresh salmon and half smoked salmon.

 10 min   10 min   easy 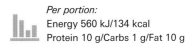 6 portions

Per portion:
Energy 560 kJ/134 kcal
Protein 10 g/Carbs 1 g/Fat 10 g

QUICK CHEESE SOUFFLÉS

INGREDIENTS

50 g butter, cut into pieces,
    plus extra for greasing
60 g flour, plus extra for dusting
150 g Gruyère cheese,
    cut into pieces
4 eggs
300 g milk
1 pinch ground nutmeg
½ tsp salt
1 pinch ground black pepper
100 g cream, min. 30% fat

USEFUL ITEMS

6 ceramic soufflé dishes
    (approx. Ø 8 cm, height 4.5 cm)

PRÉPARATION

1. Preheat oven to 180°C. Grease and flour 6 ceramic soufflé dishes (approx. Ø 8 cm, height 4.5 cm) and set aside.
2. Place Gruyère cheese in mixing bowl and grate **10 sec/speed 7**. Transfer into a bowl and set aside.
3. Place eggs, flour, milk, butter, nutmeg, salt and black pepper into mixing bowl and heat **3 min/90°C/speed 3**.
4. Add cream and reserved grated Gruyère cheese and mix **10 sec/speed 6**. Transfer into prepared soufflé dishes and bake for 20-25 minutes (180°C) or until golden brown. Serve immediately.

TIP
• Serve with a green or mixed salad.

VARIATIONS
• Instead of making individual soufflés, bake in a large soufflé dish (Ø 20 cm) for 35-40 minutes.
• Replace Gruyère with the cheese of your choice (e.g. Parmesan, feta, Gouda, blue Stilton).
• Add fresh herbs or spices (e.g. rosemary, oregano, caraway seeds).

 10 min   45 min   easy   6

6 portions

Per portion:
Energy 1520 kJ/363 kcal
Protein 15 g/Carbs 13 g/Fat 28 g

BAKED SPINACH AND EGGS

INGREDIENTS

50 g hard cheese, for grating
    (e.g. Gruyère, Cheddar,
    Parmesan)
500 g frozen spinach leaves
    (defrosted)
1 garlic clove
50 g extra virgin olive oil
1 tsp salt
50 g flour
500 g milk
30 g butter
1 pinch ground nutmeg
1 pinch ground black pepper
6 eggs

USEFUL ITEMS

paper towel
6 ceramic soufflé dishes
    (approx. Ø 8 cm, height 4.5 cm)

PREPARATION

1. Drain spinach in Varoma. Meanwhile, place hard cheese into mixing bowl and grate **5 sec/speed 7**. Transfer grated cheese into a bowl and set aside.
2. Place garlic clove and olive oil into mixing bowl and chop **5 sec/speed 7**, then sauté **5 min/120°C/speed 2**. Meanwhile, pat spinach dry with paper towels.
3. Add spinach and salt to mixing bowl and sauté **5 min/120°C/◖/speed ◗**.
4. Preheat oven to 200°C.
5. Add flour into mixing bowl and cook **1 min 30 sec/120°C/◖/speed 2**.
6. Add milk, butter, nutmeg and black pepper and cook **7 min/100°C/speed 2**.
7. Transfer half of spinach into 6 ceramic soufflé dishes (approx. Ø 8 cm, height 4.5 cm), break one egg on top of each and cover with remaining half of spinach. Sprinkle with reserved grated cheese, bake for 10 minutes (200°C) to cook the eggs and brown the cheese topping. Serve immediately.

TIPS

- For a browner top, place soufflé dishes under a hot grill for a few minutes (but bear in mind this will extend the cooking time for the eggs).
- This dish can also be prepared in one large casserole dish.
- The creamed spinach can be prepared to the end of step 6 ahead of time. Allow spinach to cool then refrigerate. When ready to serve, proceed with step 7, adding a minute or two to the baking time.

 15 min 35 min easy  6 portions

Per portion:
Energy 1327 kJ/317 kcal
Protein 15 g/Carbs 11 g/Fat 24 g

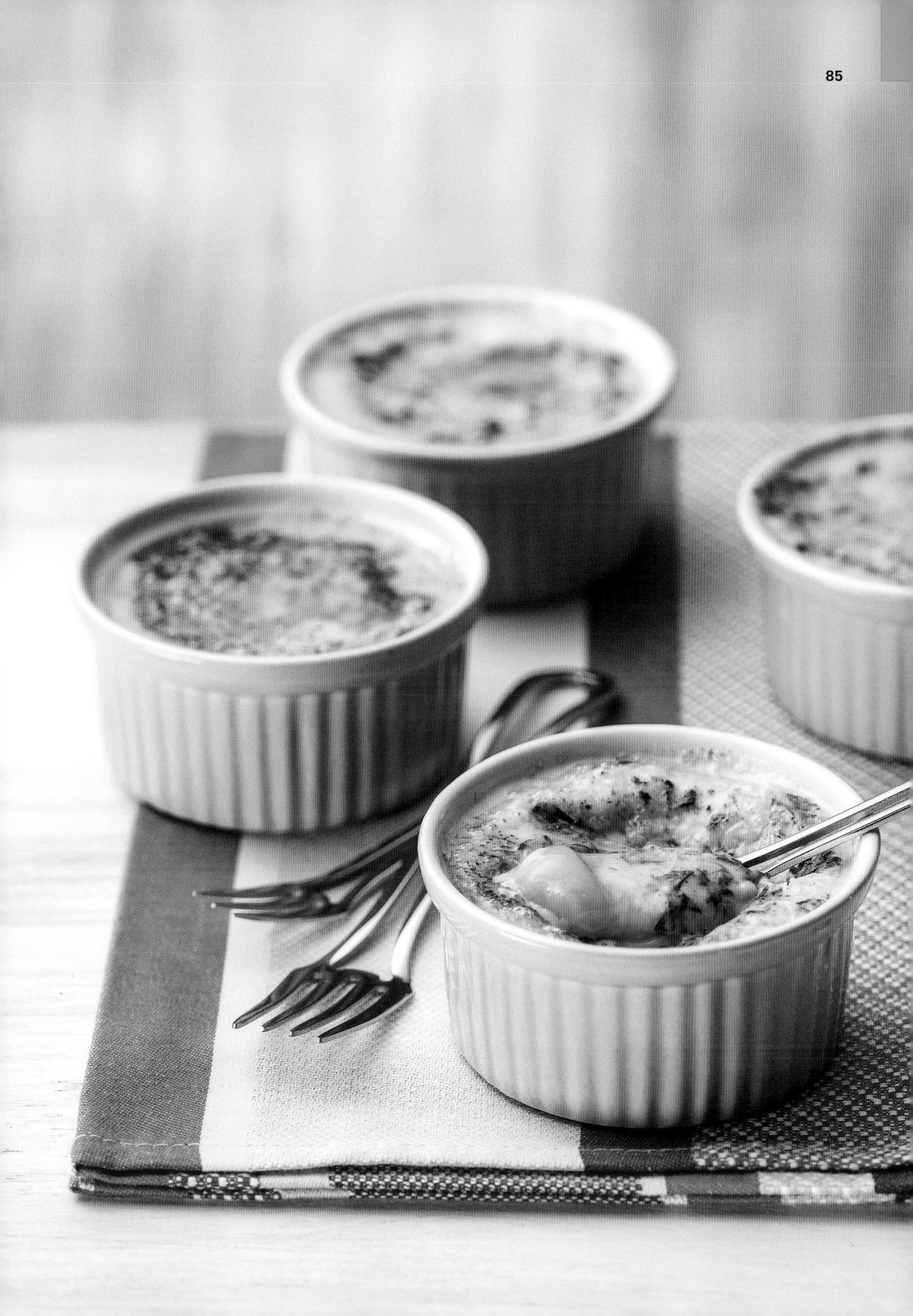

SOUPS

GAZPACHO

INGREDIENTS

1000 g plum tomatoes, ripe,
    cut into halves
50 g green peppers
40 g onions
70 g cucumber, partially peeled
1 garlic clove
30 g vinegar
1 tsp salt
50-100 g extra virgin olive oil
8 ice cubes

PREPARATION

1. Place tomatoes, green peppers, onions, cucumber, garlic clove, vinegar, salt, extra virgin olive oil and ice cubes into mixing bowl and chop **30 sec/speed 5**. Blend a further **3 min/speed 10** and refrigerate for at least an hour. Serve cold.

TIPS

- Gazpacho is a summer time soup. Using fresh, ripe tomatoes gives the gazpacho its flavour. If good quality fresh tomatoes are not available, they can be replaced with canned tomatoes, though the soup's flavour will not be as fresh.
- Serve soup with small bowls of raw vegetables (e.g. 100 g each of diced tomatoes, green peppers, onions and cucumbers) and bread, cut into small cubes, so that guests can add garnishes as they desire.
- If you prefer gazpacho without emulsifying the oil, add it after blending the other ingredients and mix **2 sec/speed 7**. Gazpacho will have a deeper red colour instead of being orange.
- Add 200 g cold water if you prefer it thinner. For thicker gazpacho, in step 1 add 150 g stale white bread, cut into pieces.

 10 min 1 h 15 min easy 6 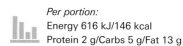 6 portions

Per portion:
Energy 616 kJ/146 kcal
Protein 2 g/Carbs 5 g/Fat 13 g

LEEK AND POTATO SOUP

INGREDIENTS

300 g leek (white part only),
   cut into pieces
1 tsp salt, plus extra to taste
30 g extra virgin olive oil
30 g butter
250 g potatoes, cut into pieces
700 g water
1 pinch ground white pepper
1 pinch ground nutmeg
100 g cream or evaporated milk
100 g milk
fresh chives, chopped (to garnish)
   or fresh flat-leaf parsley,
   chopped (to garnish)

PREPARATION

1. Place leek and salt into mixing bowl and chop **4 sec/speed 5**.
   Scrape down sides of mixing bowl with spatula.
2. Add olive oil and butter and sauté **12 min/120°C/speed 1**.
3. Add potatoes and chop **4 sec/speed 4.5**.
4. Add 600 g water and white pepper and cook **20 min/100°C/speed 1**.
   Add nutmeg, cream, milk and remaining 100 g water and blend
   1 min/speed 5-10, increasing speed gradually. Adjust
   seasoning to taste and serve hot, sprinkled with chopped fresh chives.

VARIATIONS

- Replace water with chicken stock, or add 2 tsp chicken stock paste and reduce salt.
- Instead of 100 g milk and 100 g cream, use 200 g cream for a richer soup,
  or 200 g milk for a lighter soup.
- For a more rustic texture, decrease blending time in step 5, or omit blending
  altogether.
- **Vichyssoise (cold soup):** allow soup to cool, then refrigerate for several hours.
  Adjust the seasoning to taste and serve cold, with crusty bread.

 10 min   40 min   easy    6 portions

Per portion:
Energy 742 kJ/177 kcal
Protein 3 g/Carbs 10 g/Fat 13 g

VEGETABLE SOUP

INGREDIENTS

300 g potatoes, cut into pieces
100 g tomatoes, cut into halves
80 g onions, cut into halves
1 garlic clove
400 g mixed vegetables
    (e. g. carrots, turnips, leeks),
    cut into pieces
2 sprigs fresh parsley
½ tsp salt, adjust to taste
¼-½ tsp ground pepper, to taste
600 g water, adjust to taste
20 g butter or olive oil

PREPARATION

1. Place potatoes, tomatoes, onions, garlic clove, mixed vegetables, parsley, salt, pepper and water into mixing bowl and cook **25 min/100°C/speed 1**.
2. Add butter and blend **1 min/speed 5-10, increasing speed gradually**. Serve hot.

VARIATION

• Before step 1, you can sauté onions and garlic clove in 20 g oil. Place onions, garlic clove and olive oil into mixing bowl, chop **5 sec/speed 7** and sauté **3 min/120°C/speed 1**. Proceed as directed by the recipe and omit butter in step 2.

 15 min   35 min   easy   6 portions   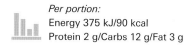

Per portion:
Energy 375 kJ/90 kcal
Protein 2 g/Carbs 12 g/Fat 3 g

CREAMY TOMATO SOUP

INGREDIENTS

1 garlic clove

50 g onions, cut into halves

30 g butter or olive oil

700 g tomatoes, cut into halves

70 g tomato purée (concentrated)

1 tsp salt

1 tsp sugar

1 tsp dried oregano or dried pizza
   herb mix

500 g water

1 stock cube (for 0.5 l) or
   1 heaped tsp stock paste,
   homemade

100 g cream

2-4 fresh basil leaves

1 sprig fresh parsley, leaves only

PREPARATION

1. Place garlic clove and onions into mixing bowl and chop
   3 sec/speed 5. Scrape down sides of mixing bowl with spatula.
2. Add butter and sauté **3 min/120°C/speed 1**.
3. Add tomatoes, tomato purée, salt, sugar and dried oregano and
   chop **5 sec/speed 5**.
4. Add water and stock cube and cook **15 min/100°C/speed 2**.
5. Add cream, basil leaves and parsley and blend
   1 min/speed 4-8, increasing speed gradually. Serve warm.

VARIATIONS

- Oregano can also be replaced with a mixture of thyme, oregano and marjoram.
  For dried herbs, use approx. 1 tsp. For fresh herbs, which have a more intense
  flavour, add sparingly and taste soup before any further additions.
- Cream can be replaced with sour cream.

 10 min   25 min   easy   4 portions

Per portion:
Energy 790 kJ/188 kcal
Protein 3 g/Carbs 9 g/Fat 16 g

CREAMY COURGETTE SOUP

INGREDIENTS

50 g onions, cut into halves

1 garlic clove (optional)

500 g courgettes, cut into pieces

500 g water

1 vegetable stock cube (for 0.5 l)
  or 1 heaped tsp vegetable stock
  paste, homemade

½ tsp salt, plus extra to taste

1 pinch ground pepper, plus extra
  to taste

10 g butter

40 g spreadable cheese
  (e.g. Laughing Cow®)

PREPARATION

1. Place onions and garlic clove into mixing bowl and chop **3 sec/speed 5**. Scrape down sides of mixing bowl with spatula.

2. Add courgettes, water, vegetable stock cube, salt and pepper and cook **15 min/100°C/speed 1**.

3. Add butter and spreadable cheese and blend **1 min/speed 4-8, increasing speed gradually**. Adjust seasoning to taste and serve immediately.

 10 min   25 min   easy   4 portions    Per portion:
Energy 354 kJ/85 kcal
Protein 4 g/Carbs 4 g/Fat 6 g

CREAMY MUSHROOM SOUP

INGREDIENTS

200 g button mushrooms

700 g water

200 g milk

1 vegetable stock cube (for 0.5 l)
or 1 heaped tsp vegetable stock
paste, homemade

50 g flour

½ tsp salt

50 g cream

4 sprigs fresh parsley, leaves only

40 g spreadable cheese
(e.g. Laughing Cow®) (optional)

PREPARATION

1. Place button mushrooms into mixing bowl and chop **5 sec/speed 4**.
2. Add water, milk, vegetable stock cube, flour and salt and cook
   10 min/100°C/speed 3.
3. Add cream, parsley and spreadable cheese and cook
   2 min/90°C/speed 2.
4. Blend **30 sec/speed 4-7, increasing speed gradually**. Serve hot.

TIP
• Garnish with a few fried button mushroom slices.

 10 min   20 min   easy   4 portions

Per portion:
Energy 523 kJ/125 kcal
Protein 5 g/Carbs 12 g/Fat 6 g

ASPARAGUS CREAM SOUP

INGREDIENTS

400 g white asparagus, peeled, woody part discarded, cut into pieces (4 cm)

100 g potatoes, cut into pieces

50 g onions, cut into halves

1 garlic clove

700 g water

1 heaped tsp vegetable stock paste, homemade, or 1 vegetable stock cube (for 0.5 l)

¼-½ tsp salt, to taste

1-2 pinches ground black pepper, to taste

50 g spreadable cheese or cream cheese

50-100 g sour cream, 20% fat or Greek yoghurt

3 sprigs fresh parsley, leaves only, chopped

PREPARATION

1. Place asparagus, potatoes, onions and garlic clove into mixing bowl and chop **7 sec/speed 5**. Scrape down sides of mixing bowl with spatula.
2. Add 300 g water, stock paste, salt and black pepper and cook **15 min/100°C/speed 2**.
3. Add cheese and sour cream and blend **30 sec/speed 3-8, increasing speed gradually**.
4. Add remaining 400 g water and cook **5 min/100°C/speed 2**. Sprinkle with parsley and serve hot.

VARIATIONS

- Parsley can be replaced with dill for a distinct flavour.
- Replace white asparagus with green asparagus.
- You can also use white asparagus from a jar, provided they are not pickled, but preserved in water-based brine.

 10 min   25 min    easy   6 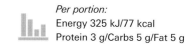 6 portions

Per portion:
Energy 325 kJ/77 kcal
Protein 3 g/Carbs 5 g/Fat 5 g

PUMPKIN SOUP

INGREDIENTS

10 g oil

10 g fresh ginger

400 g pumpkin flesh,
     cut into pieces

100 g potatoes, cut into pieces

50 g raw cashew nuts

½ tsp salt, plus extra to taste

2 pinches ground white pepper

750 g water

PREPARATION

1. Place oil and fresh ginger into mixing bowl and chop **5 sec/speed 5,** then sauté **3 min/120°C/speed 1**.
2. Add pumpkin, potato, cashew nuts, salt, white pepper and water, cook **15 min/100°C/speed 1**, then blend **1 min/speed 5-10, increasing speed gradually.**
   Adjust seasoning to taste and serve hot.

TIPS

• Select a mature pumpkin for a more aromatic and sweeter flavour.
• For a thinner soup consistency, add 150 g water and blend **20 sec/speed 7**.
• If using unpeeled pumpkin with seeds extend cooking time by 3-5 minutes in step 2 and blend for one minute longer.

 15 min   35 min   easy    4 / 4 portions

Per portion:
Energy 592 kJ/141 kcal
Protein 4 g/Carbs 12 g/Fat 9 g

CHICKPEA SOUP WITH SPINACH

INGREDIENTS

300 g fresh spinach, roughly
    chopped as necessary
100 g dried chickpeas
800 g water
1 tsp salt
200 g onions, cut into pieces (3 cm)
30 g olive oil
250 g carrots, cut into pieces (3 cm)
3 garlic cloves
100 g turnips, cut into pieces (3 cm)
    (optional)
1 pinch ground black pepper

PREPARATION

1. Place Varoma dish onto mixing bowl lid, weigh spinach into it and set aside.
2. Place dried chickpeas into mixing bowl and grind **30 sec/speed 9**.
3. Add 400 g water and mix **15 sec/speed 4**. Scrape bottom of mixing bowl with spatula.
4. Add remaining 400 g water, salt, onions, olive oil, carrots, garlic clove, turnips and black pepper. Place Varoma into position and cook **30 min/Varoma/speed 1**. Set Varoma aside.
5. Insert measuring cup and blend **1 min 30 sec/speed 4-8, increasing speed gradually**. Add spinach, combine with spatula and serve immediately.

VARIATIONS
- If you prefer to cook spinach only briefly, add it to the Varoma in the last 5-10 minutes of cooking in step 4.
- Replace fresh spinach with approx. 150 g frozen spinach. Let it defrost, then squeeze water out with your hands. Add it to the Varoma in the last 5-10 minutes of cooking in step 4.

 15 min   40 min   easy   8 portions   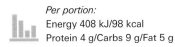 *Per portion:*
Energy 408 kJ/98 kcal
Protein 4 g/Carbs 9 g/Fat 5 g

NOODLE SOUP

INGREDIENTS

40 g onions, cut into halves
2 garlic cloves
40 g olive oil
100 g thin dried pasta for soups
   (e.g. fidelini)
250 g tomatoes, cut into pieces or
   crushed tomatoes, canned
50 g tomato purée (concentrated)
2 heaped tsp stock paste,
   homemade, meat or vegetable,
   or 2 stock cubes (each for 0.5 l)
½-1 tsp ground cumin, to taste
   (optional)
800 g water

PREPARATION

1. Place onions, garlic cloves and olive oil into mixing bowl and chop **10 sec/speed 7**, then sauté **5 min/120°C/speed 1**.
2. Add pasta and sauté **3 min/120°C/⟳/speed ⌇**. Transfer into a bowl and set aside.
3. Place tomatoes, tomato purée, stock paste and cumin into mixing bowl and blend **1 min/speed 8**.
4. Add water and heat **7 min/100°C/speed 1**.
5. Add reserved sautéed pasta and cook for **time indicated on packet/ 100°C/⟳/speed 1**. Serve immediately.

TIPS
• Increase pasta as desired to 200 g.
• If using long thin pasta, break it roughly before adding it in step 2.

  10 min   35 min   easy    6 portions

Per portion:
Energy 568 kJ/136 kcal
Protein 3 g/Carbs 14 g/Fat 7 g
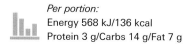

ONION SOUP

INGREDIENTS

80 g Gruyère cheese, cut into pieces
500 g onions, cut into halves
30 g olive oil
20 g butter
½ tsp salt, plus extra to taste
2 pinches ground black pepper,
     plus extra to taste
2 tsp flour (10 g)
200 g dry white wine
800 g water
1 stock cube (for 0.5 l), chicken
     or beef, or 1 heaped tsp stock
     paste, homemade
12 slices baguette, slightly stale,
     or other crusty bread

USEFUL ITEMS

6 heat-proof soup bowls

PREPARATION

1. Place Gruyère cheese into mixing bowl and grate **6 sec/speed 7**.
   Transfer into a bowl and set aside.
2. Place onions, olive oil, butter, salt and black pepper into mixing bowl
   and chop **10 sec/speed 4,** then sauté **10 min/120°C/♻/speed 1**
   without measuring cup. Scrape bottom of mixing bowl with spatula to
   loosen caramelised onions.
3. Add flour, dry white wine, water and stock cube, mix
   10 sec/♻/speed 3 then cook **20 min/100°C/♻/speed 1**.
   Adjust seasoning to taste.
4. Preheat oven grill to 210°C.
5. Pour soup into heat-proof soup bowls, place 2 baguette slices on top
   of each bowl and sprinkle with reserved grated Gruyère cheese.
   Place bowls under the grill until cheese is melted and slightly brown.
   Serve immediately.

TIP

• In step 2, the onions can be sautéed up to 15 minutes to increase caramelisation.
  Brown residue may stick to the bottom of the mixing bowl.

 10 min   1 h   medium   6 portions
Per portion:
Energy 1034 kJ/247 kcal
Protein 9 g/Carbs 28 g/Fat 8 g

MINESTRONE

INGREDIENTS

80 g onions, cut into halves

120 g leek, cut into pieces

40 g extra virgin olive oil

600 g mixed vegetables
(e.g. potatoes, carrots,
courgettes, celery stalks,
tomatoes, chard leaves,
cooked dried beans, pumpkin),
cut into pieces as needed

1000 g water

2 vegetable stock cubes
(each for 0.5 l) or
2 heaped tsp vegetable
stock paste, homemade

1 tsp salt

120 g ditalini or similar short
dried pasta

To serve

6 tsp extra virgin olive oil

6 fresh basil leaves, torn into pieces
(optional)

6-18 tsp Parmesan cheese, grated

PREPARATION

1. Place onions and leek into mixing bowl and chop **5 sec|speed 7.**
Scrape down sides of mixing bowl with spatula.

2. Add extra virgin olive oil and sauté **3 min/120°C/speed 1.**

3. Add mixed vegetables and chop **6-10 sec/speed 4.**

4. Add water and vegetable stock cubes and cook
15 min/100°C/☊/speed 1.

5. Add salt and ditalini and cook for **time indicated on packet/
100°C/☊/speed 1.** Serve soup hot, drizzled with extra virgin
olive oil and sprinkled with basil leaves and grated Parmesan cheese
to taste.

TIP
• This is a good recipe for using up leftover vegetables.

VARIATIONS
• Replace pasta with 60 g rice. Check rice packet for cooking times.
• For minestrone without pasta or rice, reduce water to 700 g in step 4 and extend
cooking time by 8 minutes.

 20 min   45 min   easy 6  6 portions *Per portion:*
Energy 1202 kJ/287 kcal
Protein 11 g/Carbs 21 g/Fat 18 g

SPICED MOROCCAN LENTIL SOUP

INGREDIENTS

150 g onions, cut into halves
40 g olive oil
1 tsp ground dried ginger
1 tsp ground coriander
1 tsp ground cumin
1 tsp sweet paprika
¼ tsp ground black pepper,
    plus extra to taste
½ tsp ground cinnamon
½ tsp ground turmeric
¼ tsp chilli powder
¼ tsp ground nutmeg
750 g water
2 heaped tsp vegetable stock paste,
    homemade, or 2 vegetable
    stock cubes (each for 0.5 l)
100 g red lentils
800 g crushed tomatoes, canned
1 pinch salt, adjust to taste
2-3 sprigs fresh coriander,
    leaves only, to garnish

PREPARATION

1. Place onions and olive oil into mixing bowl and chop **3 sec/speed 5**, then sauté **3 min/120°C/speed 1**.
2. Add ginger, coriander, cumin, sweet paprika, black pepper, cinnamon, turmeric, chilli powder and nutmeg and cook **1 min/100°C/speed 1** to release the flavours.
3. Add water, vegetable stock paste, red lentils and crushed tomatoes and cook **15-20 min/100°C/⟲/speed 1** or until lentils are cooked. Season with salt and extra black pepper to taste, garnish with fresh coriander and serve soup hot.

TIP
• Serve with fresh crusty bread.

VARIATION
• Replace red lentils with green or brown lentils. Check packet for soaking instructions. It may be necessary to increase cooking time in step 3.

 10 min
 40 min
 easy
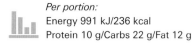 4 portions

Per portion:
Energy 991 kJ/236 kcal
Protein 10 g/Carbs 22 g/Fat 12 g

BORSCHT

INGREDIENTS

3-5 sprigs fresh parsley, leaves only
200 g tomatoes, cut into pieces
100 g onions, cut into halves
100 g carrots, cut into pieces
200 g beetroots, cut into pieces
    (2 cm)
40 g oil
150 g potatoes, cut into pieces
    (2 cm)
100 g red peppers, cut into pieces
    (2 cm)
200 g white cabbage, cut into strips
1000 g water
2 tsp salt
½ tsp ground black pepper

PREPARATION

1. Place parsley into mixing bowl and chop **3 sec/speed 7**.
2. Add tomatoes and chop **10 sec/speed 4**, then transfer into a bowl and set aside.
3. Place onions and carrots into mixing bowl and chop **5 sec/speed 5**.
4. Add beetroots and oil and sauté **5 min/Varoma/⟳/speed 1.5**.
5. Add potatoes, red peppers, white cabbage and water and cook **17 min/100°C/⟳/speed 1**.
6. Add reserved chopped tomatoes and parsley, salt and black pepper and cook **5 min/100°C/⟳/speed 1**. Allow soup to rest for 10 minutes before serving.

TIP
• Top soup with sour cream and serve with dark rye bread.

 15 min 50 min easy 6 portions 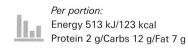 *Per portion:* Energy 513 kJ/123 kcal Protein 2 g/Carbs 12 g/Fat 7 g

MONKFISH AND PRAWN SOUP

INGREDIENTS

450-500 g monkfish, preferably
    with bone (see tips)
500 g whole unpeeled prawns
    (see tips)
800 g water
70 g carrots, cut into pieces
60 g leek (white part only),
    cut into pieces
3 garlic cloves
50 g extra virgin olive oil
50 g brandy
200 g crushed tomatoes, canned
1 tbsp white short-grain rice
1 pinch saffron threads
1 fish stock cube (for 0.5 l) (see tip)
    or 1 tsp salt
8 drops chilli sauce (optional)

PREPARATION

1. Cut monkfish into pieces (2-3 cm) and set aside. Cut monkfish bone into pieces (2 cm) and place into mixing bowl. Peel and set aside prawns, reserving shells and heads.

2. Add prawn shells, prawn heads and 500 g water into mixing bowl and cook **7 min/100°C/speed 1**. Strain fish stock through simmering basket over a bowl and set aside. Discard monkfish bones, prawn shells and prawns heads.

3. Rinse mixing bowl. Place carrots, leek, garlic clove and extra virgin olive oil into mixing bowl and chop **3 sec/speed 5**, then sauté **6 min/120°C/speed 1**.

4. Add brandy and reduce **1 min/Varoma/speed 1** without measuring cup to help alcohol evaporation.

5. Add crushed tomatoes and rice and sauté **5 min/120°C/speed 1**.

6. Add saffron, stock cube, 200 g water and reserved fish stock and cook **7 min/100°C/speed 1**.

7. Add 100 g water and blend **30 sec/speed 5-10, increasing speed gradually**, then cook **3 min/100°C/speed 1**.

8. Add reserved prawns, reserved monkfish and chilli sauce and heat **1 min/100°C/⟲/speed ◁**. Serve hot.

TIPS

- You can use frozen monkfish and prawns, allowing them to defrost first.
- The monkfish bone, prawn heads and prawn shells give the fish stock its flavour. If your monkfish is sold without the bone, and if your prawns are small or don't have heads, use 2 fish stock cubes instead of 1. If you have a monkfish bone and large prawns with heads, you can omit the stock cube and use salt instead.

 30 min   1 h   medium   6 6 portions    Per portion: Energy 791 kJ/189 kcal Protein 18 g/Carbs 5 g/Fat 10 g

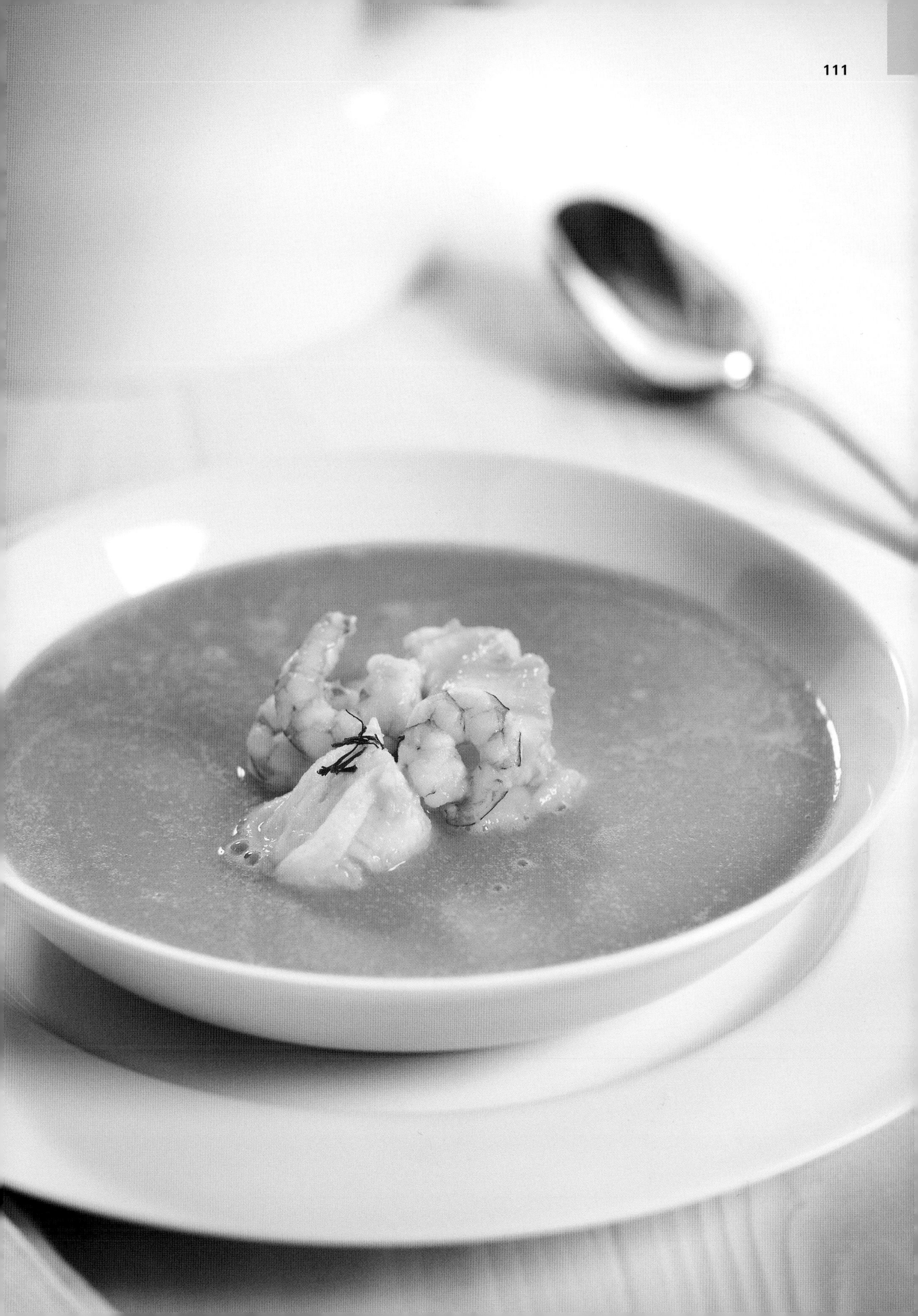

PASTA AND RICE DISHES

SPAGHETTI CARBONARA

INGREDIENTS

60 g Parmesan cheese,
    cut into pieces
30 g pecorino cheese (optional)
1 shallot (30 g)
150 g bacon cubes
20 g extra virgin olive oil
1200 g water
¾ tsp salt
350 g spaghetti
3 eggs
1 egg yolk
2 pinches ground black pepper

PREPARATION

1. Place Parmesan and pecorino cheese into mixing bowl and grate **10 sec/speed 10**. Transfer into a bowl and set aside.
2. Place shallot into mixing bowl and chop **3 sec/speed 5**. Scrape down sides of mixing bowl with spatula.
3. Add bacon cubes and extra virgin olive oil and sauté **5 min/120°C/speed 1**. Transfer into a large serving bowl and keep warm.
4. Place water and ½ tsp salt into mixing bowl and bring to a boil **10 min/100°C/speed 1**.
5. Add spaghetti through hole in the mixing bowl lid and cook without measuring cup for **time indicated on packet/100°C/⟲/speed 1** or until al dente. Drain spaghetti through Varoma dish and transfer into serving bowl with bacon. Mix well and keep warm.
6. Before pasta has a chance to cool, place eggs, egg yolk, reserved grated cheese, ¼ tsp salt and black pepper into mixing bowl and mix **15 sec/speed 4**. Add egg mixture into serving bowl with pasta and bacon. Combine thoroughly with spatula and serve immediately.

TIPS
- If water bubbles into mixing bowl lid while pasta is cooking, add 1 tsp oil or butter to the cooking water to reduce frothing.
- Pasta that is cooked al dente is tender but still firm to the bite.
- The heat of the cooked pasta will partially cook and thicken the egg, so it is important the pasta is still hot when adding the egg mixture to the serving bowl.
- To ensure the eggs are not overcooked and the sauce is creamy, in step 6 you can rinse the mixing bowl in cold water to cool it off before adding the eggs.

 10 min   35 min easy   4 portions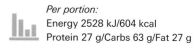
Per portion:
Energy 2528 kJ/604 kcal
Protein 27 g/Carbs 63 g/Fat 27 g

TAGLIATELLE WITH SAUTÉED PORCINI MUSHROOMS

INGREDIENTS

20 g fresh parsley, leaves only

1 garlic clove

50 g extra virgin olive oil

100 g fresh porcini mushrooms, cut into slices or 30 g dried porcini mushrooms, soaked in warm water for 20 minutes, drained

1¼ tsp salt

1200 g water

300 g tagliatelle (long dried egg pasta)

1-2 pinches freshly ground black pepper, to taste

PREPARATION

1. Place parsley into mixing bowl and chop **3 sec/speed 7**. Remove 1 tbsp chopped parsley, place into a bowl and set aside. Leave remainder in mixing bowl.
2. Add garlic clove and 30 g extra virgin olive oil and sauté **3 min/120°C/speed 1**. Remove garlic clove if desired.
3. Add porcini mushrooms and ¼ tsp salt into mixing bowl and cook **12 min/100°C/◐/speed ◢**. Transfer into a serving bowl and keep warm.
4. Place water into mixing bowl and bring to a boil **10 min/100°C/speed 1**.
5. Add tagliatelle and remaining 1 tsp salt and cook without measuring cup for **time indicated on packet/100°C/◐/speed 1** or until al dente. Drain pasta through Varoma dish, then transfer into serving bowl with reserved porcini mushrooms. Add remaining 1½ tbsp extra virgin olive oil (20 g), black pepper and reserved chopped parsley and combine with spatula. Serve hot.

TIPS
- The quantity of salt can be increased to taste depending on the quality of the mushrooms.
- Serve with grated Parmesan cheese.
- Porcini mushrooms are also known as ceps.

VARIATION
- You can also make this dish with homemade pasta. Cook pasta in a saucepan while sautéing porcini mushrooms in the Thermomix™.

 25 min   1 h   easy 4 / 4 portions  Per portion: Energy 1599 kJ/382 kcal Protein 11 g/Carbs 54 g/Fat 14 g

PASTA IN TOMATO SAUCE WITH HAM AND CHORIZO

INGREDIENTS

70 g Parmesan cheese, cut into
   pieces (3 cm)

100 g dry-cured ham, e.g. Serrano
   ham, cut into cubes (1 cm)

100 g chorizo, cut into thick slices
   (1 cm)

120 g onions, cut into halves

30 g extra virgin olive oil

400 g canned tomatoes
   (whole, in juice)

½ tsp salt

½ tsp dried oregano (optional)

600 g water

350 g penne or similar short dried
   pasta

PREPARATION

1. Place Parmesan cheese into mixing bowl and grate **10 sec/speed 10**. Transfer into a bowl and set aside.
2. Place ham and chorizo into mixing bowl and chop **Turbo/0.5 sec/6-8 times**. Transfer into a bowl and set aside.
3. Place onions and olive oil into mixing bowl and chop **4 sec/speed 5**. Sauté **7 min/120°C/speed 1**.
4. Add canned tomatoes (including juice) and cook **6 min/Varoma/speed 1**.
5. Add reserved chopped ham and chorizo, salt, oregano and water and cook **4 min/100°C/speed 1**.
6. Add penne and cook for **time indicated on packet/100°C/↻/speed 1** or until al dente. Serve immediately with reserved Parmesan cheese.

VARIATION
• Place pasta into an oven dish, sprinkle with Parmesan cheese and place under the preheated oven grill until cheese is melted and golden brown.

 15 min 35 min easy 6 portions

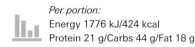

Per portion:
Energy 1776 kJ/424 kcal
Protein 21 g/Carbs 44 g/Fat 18 g

PASTA SALAD WITH TROUT AND VEGETABLES

INGREDIENTS

1000 g water

200 g white wine

100 g orange juice, freshly squeezed

1½ tsp salt

400 g trout fillets or salmon fillets, skinless

200 g frozen green peas

240 g short dried pasta (e.g. mezze penne rigate), 10 minutes cooking time

40 g extra virgin olive oil

1 garlic clove

30 g salted capers, rinsed

80 g black olives, pitted

350 g cherry tomatoes, cut into halves or quarters

1 pinch ground black pepper (optional)

10 g lemon juice (optional)

USEFUL ITEMS

large serving bowl

PREPARATION

1. Place water, wine, orange juice and salt into mixing bowl. Place trout fillets into Varoma dish and frozen green peas onto Varoma tray. Place Varoma into position and steam **12 min/Varoma/speed 1**. Set Varoma aside.

2. Add pasta through hole in mixing bowl lid and return Varoma to position. **Cook 10 min/Varoma/↻/speed 1**. Set Varoma aside and drain pasta through simmering basket, briefly rinsing it under cold water to stop cooking. Place pasta into a large serving bowl and stir in 1 tbsp extra virgin olive oil (approx. 10 g).

3. Without cleaning mixing bowl, place garlic clove and remaining 30 g extra virgin olive oil into mixing bowl and sauté **3 min/120°C/speed 1**. Remove garlic clove if desired.

4. Add steamed trout fillets, steamed peas, capers and black olives and cook **3 min/100°C/↻/speed 1**. Transfer onto pasta, add cherry tomatoes and combine. Season to taste with black pepper and lemon juice and serve at room temperature or chilled.

TIPS

• If frozen green peas are not available, they can be replaced canned green peas, drained: add them at the end of step 2 into the serving bowl with pasta and extra virgin olive oil.

• Garnish with chopped parsley, to taste.

VARIATIONS

• Trout can also be replaced with swordfish fillets. Depending on the quality and type of fish, steaming time in step 1 can be adjusted to your preference.

• If you prefer bigger pieces of fish, don't add fish into the mixing bowl in step 4. Instead, cut fish into pieces and gently combine into the salad with the spatula.

• If you prefer a stronger garlic flavour, rather than removing the garlic clove, chop it **5 sec/speed 6** in step 3 before sautéing.

 20 min   45 min   easy  6 portions

Per portion:
Energy 1497 kJ/357 kcal
Protein 21 g/Carbs 35 g/Fat 14 g

LASAGNE BOLOGNESE

INGREDIENTS

100-200 g Parmesan cheese,
cut into pieces (3 cm)

Bolognese sauce

200 g mixed vegetables
(celery stalk, carrots and
onions), cut into pieces
40 g extra virgin olive oil
800 g mixed minced meat
(half pork and half beef)
100 g dry white wine
300 g crushed tomatoes, canned
1-1½ tsp salt, to taste
½-1 tsp ground black pepper,
to taste

Béchamel sauce

1000 g milk
80 g butter, cut into pieces
100 g flour
1 tsp salt
1-2 pinches ground nutmeg

Lasagne assembly

butter, for greasing and topping
250 g dried lasagne pasta,
approx. 12 sheets
(10 cm x 20 cm)

USEFUL ITEMS

casserole dish
(approx. 30 cm x 24 cm x 6 cm)

PREPARATION

1. Place Parmesan cheese into mixing bowl and grate **15 sec/speed 10**. Transfer into a bowl and set aside. Rinse mixing bowl.

Bolognese sauce

2. Place mixed vegetables and extra virgin olive oil into mixing bowl. Chop **5 sec/speed 7**, then sauté **5 min/120°C/speed 2**.
3. Add mixed minced meat, stir with spatula to break it up if necessary, and sauté **8 min/120°C/↺/speed 1**.
4. Add dry white wine and cook **5 min/Varoma/↺/speed 1**.
5. Add crushed tomatoes, salt and black pepper and cook **20 min/100°C/↺/speed ◀**. Transfer into a bowl and set aside.

Béchamel sauce

6. Place milk, butter, flour, salt and nutmeg into mixing bowl and cook **12 min/100°C/speed 3**.

Lasagne assembly

7. Preheat oven to 180°C. Lightly grease a casserole dish and set aside.
8. Cover base of casserole dish with a thin layer of Bolognese sauce. Place a layer of dried lasagne pasta sheets over the sauce, cover with another layer of Bolognese sauce, sprinkle with some of the Parmesan cheese and cover with a layer of béchamel sauce. Repeat this step until all ingredients are used. Finish with a layer of béchamel sauce, sprinkle with remaining Parmesan cheese and dot with small pieces of butter.
9. Bake for 30-40 minutes (180°C). Allow lasagne to rest for 15-20 minutes before cutting into squares and serving.

Continued on page **124** ▶

 40 min   2 h 30 min   advanced   6 portions

Per portion:
Energy 4161 kJ/994 kcal
Protein 50 g/Carbs 53 g/Fat 64 g

► Lasagne Bolognese, continued

Step 8

TIPS

- This is a good dish for entertaining guests as it can be prepared ahead of time and baked when guests arrive.
- Usually dried lasagne pasta sheets do not need to be boiled before baking (check packet instructions). If you prefer cooking the pasta in the traditional method, pre-cook lasagne pasta sheets in a large saucepan of salted boiling water (approx. 1 tsp salt per litre of water) for approx. 5 minutes. Drain in Varoma dish and blot excess moisture by placing lasagne pasta sheets in a single layer on top of a kitchen towel. Prepare the pasta while the béchamel sauce is cooking.
- Leftovers keep well in the freezer.

VARIATIONS

- To use freshly minced meat, freeze pieces (3 cm) of sinew-free meat in a single layer for 30 minutes. Place partially-frozen meat into mixing bowl and mince **10-15 sec/speed 6**.
- Instead of dried lasagne pasta sheets use homemade fresh egg pasta.

RISOTTO WITH PARMESAN CHEESE

INGREDIENTS

40 g Parmesan cheese,
  cut into pieces (3 cm)
1 shallot (approx. 30 g)
40 g butter
10 g extra virgin olive oil
320 g risotto rice
  (e.g. Carnaroli, Arborio),
  14-15 minutes cooking time
  (see tip)
60 g dry white wine
720 g water
1 stock cube (for 0.5 l), meat or
  vegetable, or 1 heaped tsp
  stock paste, homemade
½-1 tsp salt, to taste

PREPARATION

1. Place Parmesan cheese into mixing bowl and grate **10 sec/speed 10**. Transfer into a bowl and set aside.
2. Place shallot into mixing bowl and chop **5 sec/speed 5**. Scrape down sides of mixing bowl with spatula.
3. Add 20 g butter and extra virgin olive oil and sauté **3 min/120°C/speed 1**.
4. Add risotto rice and sauté **3 min/120°C/⟳/speed 1** without measuring cup.
5. Add dry white wine and cook **1 min/100°C/⟳/speed 1** without measuring cup.
6. Add water, stock cube and salt and scrape bottom of mixing bowl with spatula to loosen rice. Cook **12-13 min/100°C/⟳/speed 1**, placing simmering basket instead of measuring cup onto mixing bowl lid to help prevent splashing. Allow risotto to rest in mixing bowl for 1 minute, then transfer into a serving bowl. Using spatula, combine with remaining 20 g butter and reserved Parmesan cheese and serve immediately.

Continued on page **126** ▶

 10 min   25 min   easy  4 portions

Per portion:
Energy 1812 kJ/433 kcal
Protein 9 g/Carbs 63 g/Fat 15 g

► Risotto with Parmesan cheese, continued

TIPS
- Risotto is best served immediately.
- Adjust cooking time according to time indicated on rice packet.
- Liquid absorption may vary according to the type of rice. If risotto seems dry before it is cooked through, add more liquid.
- Rule of thumb for creating your own risotto recipe: for every 100 g risotto rice you will need 250 g liquids (water and wine) combined with stock paste. The maximum quantity of rice that can be cooked at any one time for this basic recipe is 500 g. Bear in mind adding other ingredients (e.g. mushrooms or sausage) will add volume to the dish, so adapt rice quantity accordingly.

VARIATIONS
- **Saffron risotto:** add 2 pinches saffron in step 6.
- **Mushroom risotto:** in step 3, add 250 g fresh mushrooms (cut into pieces if too large) or 50 g dried mushrooms (soaked in water for 30 minutes, water squeezed out). Proceed as directed by recipe. Saffron can also be added in this variation.
- **Sausage and apple risotto:** in step 3, add 150 g sausage meat (cut open a fresh sausage and crumble in the minced meat). In step 4, add 100 g green apple, cut into cubes.

ASIAN-STYLE RICE WITH EGGS AND VEGETABLES

INGREDIENTS

20 g light sesame oil or peanut oil

100 g onions, cut into halves

150 g carrots, cut into large pieces (4 cm)

150 g bacon cubes

30 g soy sauce

2 tsp sugar

1 heaped tsp stock paste, homemade, or 1 stock cube (for 0.5 l) (optional)

350 g short-grain rice or long-grain rice (18-20 min cooking time)

1200 g water

400 g mixed vegetables (e.g. broccoli in small florets, frozen peas, cauliflower in small florets, green beans cut into pieces, courgettes cut into pieces)

4 eggs

PREPARATION

1. Place light sesame oil and onions into mixing bowl and chop **3 sec/speed 5**.
2. Add carrots and chop roughly **2 sec/speed 4.5**.
3. Add bacon cubes, soy sauce and sugar and sauté **7 min/120°C/speed ◁** without measuring cup. Transfer into a large serving bowl, cover and set aside.
4. Place stock paste into mixing bowl. Insert simmering basket and weigh rice into it. Add water over rice into mixing bowl. Place Varoma into position, weigh vegetables into it and close Varoma lid. Steam **14 min/Varoma/speed 2**. Meanwhile, line Varoma tray with damp baking paper. Whisk eggs in a small bowl.
5. Carefully open Varoma, stir vegetables to ensure even cooking, insert prepared Varoma tray and place whisked eggs into it. Steam **6-7 min/Varoma/speed 2**.
6. Remove Varoma, remove simmering basket with spatula and transfer rice and vegetables into serving bowl with reserved bacon mixture. Using the spatula, cut eggs into squares (2-3 cm) in the Varoma tray and transfer into serving bowl. Using the spatula, combine all ingredients in serving bowl and serve hot.

USEFUL ITEMS

large serving bowl

baking paper

VARIATIONS

- This dish can be varied endlessly according the vegetables you have on hand. Place the vegetables that require the longest cooking time first in the Varoma dish, and the others a few minutes later.
- If one ingredient isn't fully cooked, transfer the others to the serving bowl and continue to steam remaining ingredient for **a few minutes/Varoma/speed 2** before combining with ingredients in serving bowl.
- If you only have dark sesame oil (from toasted sesame seeds), use peanut oil or another mild cooking oil in step 1 and add 1 tsp dark sesame oil for flavour. Or omit sesame oil entirely.
- Replace the soy sauce and sugar with either 60 g soy paste or 60 g hoisin sauce, or omit entirely.
- Use any type of rice, making sure to adapt cooking time according to packet instructions. For instance for basmati rice, reduce steaming time in step 5 to 12 minutes.
- You can mix in chopped herbs, spring onions or nuts before serving.

 15 min 30 min medium 6  6 portions

Per portion:
Energy 1748 kJ/418 kcal
Protein 16 g/Carbs 54 g/Fat 15 g

RICE SALAD

INGREDIENTS

2 eggs

280 g courgettes,
    cut into small cubes

120 g carrots, cut into small cubes

100 g frozen green peas

1200 g water

1 tsp salt, plus extra to taste

250 g parboiled rice
    (approx. 15 minutes
    cooking time)

200 g canned tuna in oil
    (weight includes oil),
    drained, cut into pieces

100 g black or green olives,
    pitted, whole or chopped

15-20 g pickled gherkins,
    cut into slices

1 sprig fresh mint, leaves only

1 tbsp extra virgin olive oil

1-2 tsp vinegar or lemon juice
    (optional)

7 cherry tomatoes, cut into
    halves or quarters

USEFUL ITEMS

large serving bowl

PREPARATION

1. Place eggs into Varoma dish and place courgettes, carrots and frozen green peas onto Varoma tray. Set aside.
2. Place water and salt into mixing bowl, insert simmering basket and weigh rice into it. Mix rice with spatula to wet all grains for even cooking. Place Varoma into position and steam **21 min/Varoma/speed 2**. Set Varoma aside and allow eggs and vegetables to cool. Quickly rinse simmering basket with rice under cold water, then set aside to drain.
3. Pour rice into a large serving bowl, add reserved cooked vegetables, tuna, olives, pickled gherkins and mint leaves. Add extra virgin olive oil and vinegar, combine, and adjust seasoning. Peel boiled eggs and cut into slices. Garnish salad with sliced eggs and cherry tomatoes and serve at room temperature or chilled.

VARIATIONS

- Replace mint with parsley.
- Add other ingredients to taste (e.g. sliced Frankfurt sausages, sweetcorn, mozzarella cubes).

 20 min 1 h easy  4 portions

Per portion:
Energy 2027 kJ/485 kcal
Protein 21 g/Carbs 59 g/Fat 18 g

MAIN DISHES

CHICKEN WITH CREAMY VEGETABLE SAUCE

INGREDIENTS

600 g water
130 g carrots, cut into pieces
60 g celeriac, cut into pieces
60 g celery leaves or 50 g fresh
  parsley, leaves only
1 chicken stock cube (for 0.5 l)
  or 1 heaped tsp chicken stock
  paste, homemade
600 g chicken breasts, skinless,
  cut into strips (5 cm x 2 cm)
½ tsp salt, plus extra to taste
¼ tsp freshly ground pepper,
  plus extra to taste
150 g button mushrooms,
  cut into slices
40 g flour
100 g cream
1 tsp Worcestershire sauce
  (optional)
1 tsp lemon juice
60 g butter, cut into pieces

PREPARATION

1. Place water, carrots, celeriac, celery leaves and chicken stock cube into mixing bowl. Season chicken breast strips with salt and pepper and place into Varoma dish. Place Varoma into position and cook **20 min/Varoma/speed 1**. Meanwhile, place sliced button mushrooms onto Varoma tray and set aside.

2. **Carefully** open Varoma lid away from you and flip chicken strips with spatula to ensure chicken is thoroughly cooked. Insert Varoma tray with button mushrooms, close Varoma lid and cook for a further **5 min/Varoma/speed 1**. Set Varoma aside.

3. Add flour, cream, Worcestershire sauce and lemon juice into mixing bowl and cook **1 min/100°C/speed 6**.

4. Add cooked button mushroom slices and butter and cook **1 min/80°C/ ⟲/speed 2**. Adjust seasoning to taste and serve chicken and sauce separately or pour sauce over chicken before serving.

TIP
• Serve with rice or dumplings.

VARIATION
• Substitute cream with sour cream.

---

 30 min   50 min   medium   4 portions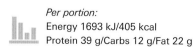

Per portion:
Energy 1693 kJ/405 kcal
Protein 39 g/Carbs 12 g/Fat 22 g

CHICKEN BREASTS PIZZAIOLA

INGREDIENTS

800 g chicken breasts, skinless
½ tsp salt, adjust to taste
½ tsp ground black pepper,
    adjust to taste
200 g Edam cheese or other
    semi-hard cheese (e.g. Gruyère,
    Emmental, Fontina), cut into
    pieces
30 g olive oil
150 g onions, cut into halves
2 garlic cloves
600 g chopped tomatoes,
    canned or fresh
1 heaped tsp stock paste,
    homemade, or 1 vegetable
    stock cube (for 0.5 l)
1 tsp sugar
1½ tsp dried oregano

USEFUL ITEMS

casserole dish

PREPARATION

1. Place chicken breasts into Varoma dish, season with salt and pepper and set aside.
2. Place Edam cheese into mixing bowl and grate **5-10 sec/speed 5**. Transfer into a bowl and set aside.
3. Preheat oven to 200°C.
4. Place olive oil, onions and garlic cloves into mixing bowl, chop **5 sec/speed 5**, then sauté **5 min/120°C/speed 1**.
5. Add tomatoes, vegetable stock paste and sugar, place Varoma into position and steam **25 min/Varoma/speed 1**.
6. Place chicken breasts into a casserole dish, cover with tomato sauce and reserved grated Edam cheese and sprinkle with oregano. Bake for 10 minutes (200°C) or until cheese becomes golden brown. Serve hot.

TIP
• Serve with potatoes, vegetables or rice: steam potatoes (cut into small cubes) or vegetables (e.g. broccoli cut into florets) together with chicken in Varoma. Or cook rice in Thermomix™ while chicken is baking.

 10 min   55 min   easy   6 portions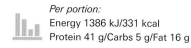

Per portion:
Energy 1386 kJ/331 kcal
Protein 41 g/Carbs 5 g/Fat 16 g

SHREDDED CHICKEN IN TOMATO SAUCE (TINGA DE POLLO)

INGREDIENTS

200 g panela cheese (Mexican fresh cheese) or feta cheese, cut into pieces

300 g onions, cut into halves

500 g tomatoes, cut into pieces

30 g oil

2 heaped tsp stock paste, homemade, or 2 stock cubes (each for 0.5 l)

1000 g chicken breasts, skinless, cut into pieces (3-4 cm)

30 g piloncillo, cut into pieces (see tip) or brown sugar

20-30 g chipotle chillies, preserved (see tip), to taste or 1 fresh chilli, deseeded, chopped

2 dried bay leaves

18 Mexican tostadas or taco shells

250 g sour cream

PREPARATION

1. Place panela cheese into mixing bowl and grate **10 sec/speed 5**. Transfer into a bowl and set aside for serving.
2. Place onions, tomatoes, oil and stock paste into mixing bowl and chop **5 sec/speed 5**, then sauté **5 min/120°C/speed 1**.
3. Add chicken breasts, piloncillo, chipotle chillies and bay leaves and cook **18 min/100°C/⟳/speed 1**, then shred **5 sec/⟳/speed 4**.
4. Serve immediately on tostadas, topped with reserved grated cheese and sour cream.

TIPS

• Piloncillo is unrefined cane sugar, produced in cone shapes. It is also known as panela (not to be confused with panela cheese). Piloncillo can sometimes be found in health food stores.

• Chipotle chillies have a smoky flavour. If you can't find any, replace with fresh chillies, adjusting amount to taste.

 10 min   30 min   easy   6 portions

Per portion:
Energy 2417 kJ/576 kcal
Protein 50 g/Carbs 34 g/Fat 26 g

CHICKEN GARAM MASALA

INGREDIENTS

Garam masala spice mix

2 tsp black peppercorns

2 tbsp coriander seeds

1 tbsp cumin seeds or caraway
   seeds

½ tsp ground nutmeg

1 tsp cloves

1 tbsp ground cardamom

½ tsp ground cinnamon

1 dried bay leaf

Chicken garam masala

400 g crushed tomatoes, canned

80 g sour cream, 10% fat

50 g butter

1 tsp sugar (optional)

½ tsp salt

500 g chicken breasts, skinless,
   cut into cubes (3 cm)

¼ tsp salt, to season chicken

USEFUL ITEMS

air-tight jar

PREPARATION

Garam masala spice mix

1. Place black peppercorns, coriander seeds, cumin seeds, nutmeg, cloves, cardamom, cinnamon and bay leaf into mixing bowl and grind **40 sec/speed 10**. Transfer into an air-tight jar and set aside.

Chicken garam masala

2. Place crushed tomatoes, sour cream, butter and sugar into mixing bowl and cook **12 min/100°C/speed 2**, placing simmering basket instead of measuring cup onto mixing bowl lid to help prevent splashing.

3. Add salt and 2 tbsp reserved garam masala spice mix and cook **3 min/Varoma/speed 1**, placing simmering basket instead of measuring cup onto mixing bowl lid to help prevent splashing.

4. Add chicken breasts and salt into mixing bowl, insert measuring cup and cook **6 min/100°C/↺/speed ⟳**. Add salt to taste and serve hot.

TIPS

• Serve with basmati or plain rice and sprinkle with parsley.

• Serve with plain yoghurt if you wish to tone down the spiciness.

• Reserve the rest of the garam masala spice mix for another curry recipe.

VARIATION

• For a faster version replace the garam masala spice mix with a store-bought version.

---

 10 min
 50 min
 easy
 4 portions plus additional spice mix
 Per portion: Energy 1159 kJ/277 kcal Protein 32 g/Carbs 5 g/Fat 14 g

QUICK THAI CHICKEN CURRY

INGREDIENTS

1 garlic clove
50-100 g onions
½-1 tsp salt
30 g oil
50-100 g Thai red curry paste
200 g coconut milk
200 g water
400 g waxy potatoes, peeled,
    cut into bite-size pieces
100 g carrots, cut into bite-size
    pieces
600 g chicken breasts, skinless,
    cut into cubes (3 cm)
150 g frozen green peas
2-3 sprigs fresh coriander,
    leaves only, to garnish

PREPARATION

1. Place garlic clove, onions, salt and oil into mixing bowl and chop **3 sec/speed 5**.
2. Add Thai curry paste and sauté **3 min/120°C/speed 1**.
3. Add coconut milk, water, potatoes and carrots and cook **12 min/100°C/◓/speed 1**.
4. Add chicken breasts and frozen green peas and cook **8 min/100°C/◓/speed 1**. Garnish with coriander leaves and serve hot.

TIP
- Serve with rice.

VARIATION
- In step 3, add flavourings such as 15 g fish sauce, 2 tsp sugar, and/or 2-3 kaffir lime leaves.
- Just before serving, add 20 g lime juice, 5-6 fresh basil leaves (if possible Thai basil) and/or 1 fresh chilli, cut into thin slices.
- Replace the potatoes, carrots and peas with any vegetables of your choice, cut into bite-size pieces as needed. Add the longer-cooking vegetables (e.g. aubergines, sweet potatoes, squash) in step 3, and faster-cooking vegetables (e.g. broccoli, cauliflower, green beans, snow peas, cherry tomatoes, courgettes, sweetcorn) in step 4 or a few minutes before the end of the cooking time.
- Replace chicken breasts with quick-cooking boneless meat of your choice, for instance turkey breasts or pork tenderloin.

 20 min   40 min   easy   4 portions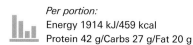
Per portion:
Energy 1914 kJ/459 kcal
Protein 42 g/Carbs 27 g/Fat 20 g

PORK TENDERLOIN WITH MUSTARD SAUCE

INGREDIENTS

450 g pork tenderloin,
      cut into slices (1 cm)
100 g button mushrooms,
      cut into slices
75 g white dry vermouth or
      Madeira wine
100 g milk
60 g onions, cut into halves
1 garlic clove (optional)
2 tsp wholegrain mustard
1 tsp hot mustard
1 heaped tsp chicken stock paste,
      homemade, or 1 chicken stock
      cube (for 0.5 l)
1 tsp salt
1 pinch ground black pepper,
      adjust to taste
2 tbsp crème fraîche or cream
1 heaped tbsp cornflour (starch)
2-3 sprigs fresh parsley, to garnish

PREPARATION

1. Place pork tenderloin and mushrooms into simmering basket, alternating layers of meat and layers of mushrooms. Set aside.
2. Place vermouth, milk, onions, garlic clove, wholegrain mustard, hot mustard, chicken stock paste, salt and black pepper into mixing bowl. Insert simmering basket and cook **10 min/100°C/speed 1**.
3. Stir contents of simmering basket with spatula to ensure even cooking. Cook a further **5 min/100°C/speed 1**. Meat should be cooked evenly without being dry. If necessary stir again with spatula and cook a further **5 min/100°C/speed 1**. Transfer pork and mushrooms to a serving dish and set aside in a warm place.
4. Add crème fraîche and cornflour into mixing bowl and cook **3 min/80°C/speed 4**. Coat meat and mushrooms with sauce, sprinkle with parsley and serve immediately.

TIP
• Cooking time depends on thickness of meat slices.

Step 1

 10 min   30 min   easy   4 / 4 portions   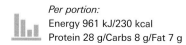 *Per portion:* Energy 961 kJ/230 kcal Protein 28 g/Carbs 8 g/Fat 7 g

BEEF GOULASH WITH BREAD DUMPLINGS

INGREDIENTS

Bread dumplings

300 g bread rolls or white bread,
  slightly stale, cut into slices
  (1 cm)
5 sprigs fresh parsley, leaves only
80 g onions, cut into halves
25 g butter, plus extra for greasing
220 g milk
3 eggs
½ tsp salt, adjust to taste
2 pinches ground black pepper
2 pinches ground nutmeg

Beef goulash and steamed dumplings

3 garlic cloves
450 g onions, cut into quarters
30 g oil or clarified butter
750 g beef (for stewing),
  cut into pieces (2-3 cm),
  patted dry with paper towels
1 tsp sugar
50 g tomato purée (concentrated)
350 g chopped tomatoes, canned
  or fresh
200 g red wine
2 tbsp sweet paprika
1 tsp salt, plus extra to taste
½ tsp ground black pepper
½ tsp ground caraway or
  caraway seeds
1 tsp grated lemon zest
1 tbsp fresh marjoram
3 dried bay leaves
5 juniper berries
1 pinch ground cloves or 2 cloves
300 g water
30 g flour
200 g peppers, red and green,
  cut into thin strips

PREPARATION

Bread dumplings

1. Place bread rolls into mixing bowl and chop **12 sec/speed 6** with aid of spatula. Transfer into a bowl and set aside.
2. Place parsley and onions into mixing bowl and chop **3 sec/speed 6**. Scrape down sides of mixing bowl with spatula.
3. Add butter and sauté **3 min/120°C/speed 1**.
4. Add milk and warm **1 min 30 sec/60°C/speed 1**.
5. Add reserved chopped bread rolls, eggs, salt, black pepper and nutmeg and mix **20 sec/⟳/speed 3** with aid of spatula. Transfer into a bowl and combine with spatula. Clean mixing bowl.

Beef goulash and steamed dumplings

6. Place garlic cloves, onions and oil into mixing bowl and chop **3 sec/speed 5**. Sauté **3 min/120°C/speed 1**.
7. Add beef and sauté **5 min/120°C/⟳/speed ⬕**.
8. Add sugar, tomato purée, chopped tomatoes, red wine, sweet paprika, salt, black pepper, caraway, lemon zest, marjoram, bay leaves, juniper berries and cloves and cook **40 min/100°C/⟳/speed 1**. Meanwhile, lightly grease Varoma dish and tray. With wet hands, form 12 dumplings from the reserved dumpling mixture and place them into greased Varoma dish and Varoma tray.
9. Add 100 g water, place Varoma with dumplings into position and steam **20 min/Varoma/⟳/speed 1**. Set Varoma aside.
10. Place a bowl onto mixing bowl lid and weigh flour and 50 g water into it. Mix flour and water.
11. Add flour-water mixture, 150 g water and peppers to mixing bowl, place Varoma back into position and cook **8 min/90°C/⟳/speed 1**. Season goulash to taste and serve hot with dumplings.

 30 min   1 h 30 min   medium   6 portions   *Per portion:* Energy 2315 kJ/553 kcal Protein 38 g/Carbs 45 g/Fat 22 g

TIPS

- Bread dumplings are best when made with day-old bread rolls, which makes this a good recipe for using up leftover rolls, baguette or sandwich bread.
- If the bread mixture is too soft to shape, add some breadcrumbs.
- Goulash can also be served with pasta, boiled potatoes or bread.

VARIATIONS

- **Bacon bread dumplings:** Add 120 g bacon cubes in step 4.
- **Venison goulash:** Replace beef with venison fillet and replace pepper strips with mushrooms (e.g. chanterelles or button mushrooms), cut into slices.

MEATBALLS WITH TOMATO SAUCE

INGREDIENTS

Meatballs

40 g bread, fresh or stale,
 cut into pieces
80 g milk
6-12 sprigs parsley, flat-leaf,
 leaves only
1 garlic clove (optional)
400 g beef mince
2 eggs
½ tsp salt
1 pinch ground black pepper
oil, for greasing

Tomato sauce

1 garlic clove
50-80 g onions, cut into halves
20 g extra virgin olive oil
600 g crushed tomatoes, canned
1 tsp salt
1 pinch ground black pepper

PREPARATION

Meatballs

1. Place a small bowl onto mixing bowl lid, weigh in bread and milk. Set bowl aside and leave to soak.
2. Place parsley and garlic clove into mixing bowl and chop **5 sec/speed 7**. Scrape down sides of mixing bowl with spatula.
3. Add beef mince, eggs, salt, and black pepper. Squeeze milk out of bread and discard milk. Add bread into mixing bowl and mix **10 sec/speed 5**. Transfer into a bowl.
4. Grease the Varoma dish and tray. With oiled hands, shape small meatballs (Ø 4 cm) and place them into Varoma dish and tray. Set aside.

Tomato sauce

5. Place garlic clove, onions and extra virgin olive oil into mixing bowl, chop **5 sec/speed 5**, then sauté **3 min/120°C/speed 1**.
6. Add crushed tomatoes, salt and black pepper. Place Varoma into position and cook **20 min/Varoma/speed 1**. Serve meatballs hot with sauce.

TIPS
- Use any white or light crusty bread such as baguette, ciabatta, country bread, whole wheat bread or bread rolls.
- Serve meatballs with rice or steamed potatoes.

VARIATIONS
- Part or all of the beef mince can be replaced with minced veal, pork or chicken.
- Add 50 g grated Parmesan cheese in step 2.
- If using fresh tomatoes, add them in step 6 and crush them **7 sec/speed 6** before continuing as directed by the recipe.

Step 4

 15 min 40 min easy 4 portions 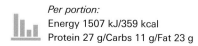 Per portion:
Energy 1507 kJ/359 kcal
Protein 27 g/Carbs 11 g/Fat 23 g

MEAT LOAF

INGREDIENTS

400 g water

6 eggs

50 g white bread, fresh or stale,
   cut into pieces

100 g milk

20 g oil, plus extra for greasing

80 g onions, cut into halves

800 g mixed minced meat
   (e.g. pork and beef)

1 tsp salt

½ tsp ground black pepper

½ tsp sweet paprika

USEFUL ITEMS

loaf tin (30 cm x 12 cm x 10 cm)

PREPARATION

1. Place water into mixing bowl, insert simmering basket and place 4 eggs into it (reserving 2 eggs for later). Steam **14 min/Varoma/speed 1**. Immediately remove simmering basket with spatula and place it with eggs under cold running water to stop cooking. Set aside.

2. Place a small bowl onto mixing bowl lid and weigh white bread and milk into bowl. Set bowl aside and leave to soak.

3. Preheat oven to 180°C. Grease a loaf tin (approx. 30 x 12 x 10 cm) and set aside.

4. Place oil and onions into mixing bowl and chop **4 sec/speed 5**. Scrape down sides of mixing bowl with spatula.

5. Sauté **3 min/120°C/speed 1**.

6. Squeeze milk out of bread and discard milk. Add bread, mixed minced meat, 2 raw eggs, salt, black pepper and sweet paprika and knead with aid of spatula **1 min/ .**

7. Transfer ⅓ of the mixture into prepared loaf tin. Peel 4 reserved hard-boiled eggs and place into loaf tin, on top of the meat mixture, distributing them along the length of the tin. Cover with the rest of the meat loaf mixture. Press firmly and smooth the surface, place into oven and bake for 40-50 minutes (180°C). Serve warm or cold.

TIPS

- Vary the spices and adjust their amount according to your preference.
- To use freshly minced meat, freeze pieces (3 cm) of sinew-free meat in a single layer for 30 minutes. Before starting the recipe, place partially-frozen meat into mixing bowl and mince **10-15 sec/speed 6**.

 15 min   1 h 20 min   easy   16 slices    *Per slice:* Energy 694 kJ/166 kcal Protein 13 g/Carbs 2 g/Fat 12 g

Step 7

STUFFED PEPPERS WITH RICE AND TOMATO SAUCE

INGREDIENTS

Stuffed peppers with rice

70 g onions, cut into halves
1 garlic clove (optional)
300 g beef mince
2 slices white bread,
    cut into pieces
20 g mustard
½ tsp salt
1 tsp sweet paprika
¼ tsp ground black pepper
1 egg
4 peppers, red, green or yellow
1200 g water
2 heaped tsp vegetable stock paste,
    homemade, or 2 vegetable
    stock cubes (each for 0.5 l)
250 g parboiled rice

Tomato sauce

40 g butter, cut into pieces
40 g flour
500 g crushed tomatoes
50 g tomato purée (concentrated)
½ tsp salt
¼ tsp ground black pepper
1 tsp sugar
1 tsp lemon juice

PREPARATION

Stuffed peppers with rice

1. Place onions and garlic clove into mixing bowl and chop **3 sec/speed 5**.
2. Add beef mince, white bread, mustard, salt, paprika, black pepper and egg and knead **1 min 30 sec/⧖**.
3. Cut the tops off the peppers and set aside. Remove all seeds and fill peppers with mince mixture, then replace cut-off top over each pepper. Place stuffed peppers into Varoma.
4. Place water and vegetable stock paste into mixing bowl, insert simmering basket and weigh rice into it. Place Varoma into position and steam **30 min/Varoma/speed 1**. Remove Varoma and remove simmering basket with aid of spatula. Transfer rice and stuffed peppers into a serving dish and keep warm. Transfer cooking liquid into a bowl and set aside.

Tomato sauce

5. Place butter and flour into mixing bowl and sauté **3 min/100°C/speed 2.**
6. Add 200 g reserved cooking liquid, crushed tomatoes, tomato purée, salt, black pepper, sugar and lemon juice and cook **5 min/100°C/speed 4**. Serve stuffed peppers with rice and tomato sauce.

TIPS
- Depending on the size of the peppers, you may have some leftover mince mixture. Form it into small balls and place them with the peppers in Varoma.
- The recipe can be halved to make two portions. But do not reduce the 1200 g water for steaming. Cooking time for the tomato sauce can be reduced by 1 minute.

VARIATION
- Instead of ground beef use ground lamb or a mixture of ground pork and beef.

---

 20 min   1 h   medium   4 portions
Per portion:
Energy 2712 kJ/648 kcal
Protein 28 g/Carbs 80 g/Fat 23 g

COTTAGE PIE

INGREDIENTS

Minced meat

100 g onions, cut into halves
20 g fresh parsley
30 g butter, plus extra for greasing
450 g beef mince
½ tsp salt
1 pinch ground black pepper,
    adjust to taste
1 tbsp Madeira wine (optional)

Mashed potatoes

900 g floury potatoes,
    cut into slices (0.5 cm)
360 g milk
1 tsp salt
1 pinch ground black pepper,
    adjust to taste
50 g butter, plus extra for topping
2 tbsp breadcrumbs or grated
    cheese (optional)

USEFUL ITEMS

casserole dish
    (approx. 22 cm x 22 cm x 10 cm)

PREPARATION

Minced meat

1. Place onions and parsley into mixing bowl and chop **5 sec/speed 5.** Scrape down sides of mixing bowl with spatula.
2. Add butter and sauté **5 min/120°C/speed 1** without measuring cup.
3. Add beef mince, salt, black pepper and Madeira wine, stir meat with spatula to break it up if necessary and cook **3 min/120°C/speed 1**. Transfer into a bowl and set aside.

Mashed potatoes

4. **Insert butterfly whisk.** Place potatoes, milk, salt and black pepper into mixing bowl and cook without measuring cup **25-30 min/98°C/speed 1**. Meanwhile, preheat oven to 220°C. Grease a casserole dish and set aside.
5. Add butter to mixing bowl, insert measuring cup and mash **30 sec/speed 3**.
6. Spread half of the mashed potatoes into the prepared casserole dish. Cover with reserved cooked minced meat mixture and spread with remaining mashed potatoes. Smooth the surface with a fork. Sprinkle with breadcrumbs and dot with butter. Bake for 15 min (220°C) or until golden brown. Serve hot.

TIP
- Serve with a green salad or steamed green peas or steamed carrots.

VARIATIONS
- The dish can be prepared in two layers. After step 5, spread the cooked minced meat mixture into the prepared casserole dish, then spread the mashed potatoes on top. Proceed as directed in step 6.
- After step 2, add 200 g carrots (cut into pieces) into mixing bowl, chop **10 sec/speed 4**, then sauté **5 min/Varoma/speed 1**. Proceed with recipe in step 3.
- Instead of raw minced meat, use leftover cooked beef, minced for a few seconds on **speed 5**.

 25 min   1 h 10 min   easy   4 portions

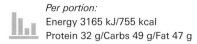
Per portion:
Energy 3165 kJ/755 kcal
Protein 32 g/Carbs 49 g/Fat 47 g

CHILLI CON CARNE

INGREDIENTS

30 g olive oil
150 g onions
1 garlic clove
250 g red peppers
200 g tomatoes, canned (whole)
  or fresh
1 fresh green chilli, deseeded,
  or ½ tsp dried chillies,
  adjust to taste
500 g beef mince
1 heaped tsp meat stock paste,
  homemade, or 1 meat stock
  cube (for 0.5 l)
1 pinch ground cumin
chilli sauce, to taste (optional)
550 g kidney beans, canned,
  drained

PREPARATION

1. Place olive oil, onions, garlic clove, peppers, tomatoes and green chilli into mixing bowl, chop **20 sec/speed 7,** then sauté **7 min/Varoma/speed 2**.
2. Add beef mince, meat stock paste, cumin and chilli sauce and cook **10 min/100°C/⟳/speed ⟱**.
3. Add beans and cook **5 min/100°C/⟳/speed ⟱**. Serve hot.

TIPS
- Serve with rice.
- If canned beans seem very firm, add beans together with beef mince in step 2, or extend cooking time in step 3 by a further **5 min/100°C/⟳/speed ⟱**.

 10 min   35 min   easy    6 portions

Per portion:
Energy 1452 kJ/346 kcal
Protein 27 g/Carbs 20 g/Fat 18 g

TROUT WITH HOLLANDAISE SAUCE

INGREDIENTS

750 g water

350 g potatoes, cut into pieces (3-4 cm)

1½ tsp salt

350 g vegetables (e.g. asparagus, cauliflower, in florets, carrots, cut into pieces)

2 fresh trout (approx. 220 g each), gutted and descaled

2 lemons (including lemon for serving)

¼ tsp ground black pepper, adjust to taste

Hollandaise sauce

100 g butter, unsalted, cut into pieces

4 egg yolks

50 g white wine

10 g lemon juice, freshly squeezed

½ tsp salt

¼ tsp ground black pepper, adjust to taste

PREPARATION

1. Place water into mixing bowl. Insert simmering basket, place potatoes into it and season with ½ tsp salt.
2. Place vegetables into Varoma dish, season with ½ tsp salt, place Varoma into position and steam **20 min/Varoma/speed 1**. Meanwhile, place trout onto Varoma tray, sprinkle with lemon juice (approx. 2 tsp) and season with black pepper and ½ tsp salt.
3. Insert Varoma tray into Varoma dish, close Varoma and steam a further **15 min/Varoma/speed 1**.
4. Check if fish, potatoes and vegetables are cooked. If not steam a further **3 min/Varoma/speed 1**. Transfer potatoes, trout and vegetables into a serving dish and keep warm. Transfer cooking liquid into a bowl. Clean mixing bowl.

Hollandaise sauce

5. **Insert butterfly whisk.** Place 50 g reserved cooking liquid, butter, egg yolks, white wine, lemon juice, salt and black pepper into mixing bowl and cook **6 min/70°C/speed 4**.
6. Serve trout immediately with sauce, lemon quarters, potatoes and vegetables.

TIP
• Adjust steaming time of vegetables in step 2 according to preference.

VARIATION
• Replace trout with other types of fish, adjusting cooking time as necessary.

 20 min 50 min medium 2 portions 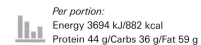 *Per portion:* Energy 3694 kJ/882 kcal Protein 44 g/Carbs 36 g/Fat 59 g

FISH AND POTATOES WITH TOMATO SAUCE

INGREDIENTS

800 g potatoes, cut into pieces (3-4 cm)

30 g olive oil, plus extra for greasing

6 hake steaks (120-200 g each) or white fish fillets (any type of white fish)

2 tsp salt, adjust to taste

150 g onions, cut into halves

1 garlic clove

100 g carrots, cut into pieces

50 g white wine (optional)

400 g tomatoes, cut into pieces

½ tsp ground black pepper

100 g water

PREPARATION

1. Place potatoes into Varoma dish and set aside. Lightly grease Varoma tray, place hake steaks onto it and season with salt to taste. Set aside.

2. Place onions, garlic clove, carrots, olive oil, white wine, tomatoes, black pepper, 1 tsp salt and water into mixing bowl and chop **5 sec/speed 5**.

3. Place Varoma without Varoma tray into position and steam **15 min/Varoma/speed 1**.

4. Insert Varoma tray into Varoma dish, close lid and steam a further **15 min/Varoma/speed 1**. Season potatoes with salt to taste. Serve hake and potatoes with the tomato sauce.

VARIATION

• For a smooth sauce, mix sauce **15 sec/speed 5** before serving.

 20 min   50 min   easy   6 portions

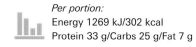

Per portion:
Energy 1269 kJ/302 kcal
Protein 33 g/Carbs 25 g/Fat 7 g

STEAMED TURBOT AND MIXED VEGETABLES PARCELS

INGREDIENTS

80 g extra virgin olive oil

¾ tsp salt

½ tsp ground black pepper

1-2 lemons, preferably organic, zest and juice

4 turbot fillets (120-200 g each) or white fish fillets (any type of white fish)

200 g mixed vegetables (e.g. carrots, courgettes, celery stalks, turnips), cut into pieces as needed

6 sprigs fresh flat-leaf parsley, leaves only

500 g water

400 g potatoes, peeled, cut into slices (3 mm)

USEFUL ITEMS

baking paper

PREPARATION

1. In a bowl mix extra virgin olive oil, ½ tsp salt, ¼ tsp pepper and 2 tbsp grated lemon zest. Add turbot fillets, coat well with marinade and allow to marinate for 30 minutes, turning fish fillets over once during that time.

2. Place mixed vegetables into mixing bowl with remaining ¼ tsp salt and remaining ¼ tsp pepper and chop **5 sec/speed 4**. Transfer into a bowl and set aside.

3. Insert simmering basket into mixing bowl and place turbot fillets and marinade inside. Once marinade has drained into mixing bowl, set simmering basket and fish fillets aside. Leave marinade mixture in mixing bowl.

4. Add parsley and approx. 50 g lemon juice and mix **10 sec/speed 5**. Transfer lemon-parsley oil into a small bowl and set aside.

5. Place turbot fillets on 4 separate squares of baking paper (30 cm x 30 cm) and distribute reserved vegetables evenly over each fillet. Fold baking paper to close packets and place parcels seam side up, 2 in Varoma dish and 2 on Varoma tray, tucking the folded ends of paper underneath the parcels.

6. Place water into mixing bowl, insert simmering basket and add potatoes. Place Varoma into position and steam **25 min/Varoma/speed 1**. Serve fish fillets immediately, their parcels partially opened, drizzled with reserved lemon-parsley oil, and with potatoes on the side.

TIP
• As the fish marinade is served as a sauce, it is important to choose high quality fish.

 20 min   1 h 15 min   easy   4 portions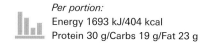
Per portion:
Energy 1693 kJ/404 kcal
Protein 30 g/Carbs 19 g/Fat 23 g

Step 5

CODFISH WITH CITRUS BUTTER

INGREDIENTS

1 orange, preferably organic,
     zest and juice
1 lemon, preferably organic,
     zest and juice
700 g water
400 g potatoes, cut into pieces
400 g courgettes,
     cut into slices (5 mm)
80 g butter, plus extra for greasing
4 codfish fillets (120-200 g each)
½ tsp salt, adjust to taste
½ tsp ground black pepper,
     adjust to taste
1 tsp aniseed seeds or fennel seeds
3 sprigs fresh parsley,
     leaves only, chopped

PREPARATION

1. Place orange and lemon zests into mixing bowl and chop **3 sec/speed 7**. Transfer into a small bowl and set aside.
2. Place water into mixing bowl, insert simmering basket and weigh potatoes into it. Place Varoma dish into position and weigh courgettes into it. Lightly grease Varoma tray. Season both sides of codfish fillets with salt and black pepper, place onto Varoma tray and sprinkle with ¼ of the reserved chopped zest. Insert Varoma tray into Varoma dish, close Varoma lid and steam **25 min/Varoma/speed 1**.
3. Remove Varoma and remove simmering basket with spatula. Transfer courgettes, fish and potatoes onto a large dish, set aside and keep warm. Empty mixing bowl.
4. Place butter, aniseed seeds and remaining citrus zests into mixing bowl and heat **4 min/60°C/speed 1**.
5. Add orange and lemon juice into mixing bowl and mix **30 sec/speed 3**. Place codfish, courgettes and potatoes onto plates. Pour over warm citrus butter, sprinkle with parsley and serve immediately.

VARIATION

• Substitute potatoes with rice: increase water to 1200 g and place 200 g rice (preferably long grain rice with 20 minutes cooking time) into simmering basket. Steam **25 min/Varoma/speed 4** and proceed as directed by the recipe.

Step 1

 25 min   50 min   easy   4 portions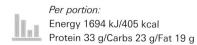
Per portion:
Energy 1694 kJ/405 kcal
Protein 33 g/Carbs 23 g/Fat 19 g

SALMON IN MUSHROOM CREAM SAUCE WITH POTATOES

INGREDIENTS

500 g water

1½ tsp salt, plus extra to taste

600 g potatoes, cut into quarters

10 g butter, plus extra for greasing

4 fresh salmon fillets, skinless
(120-200 g each, approx. 2 cm
thick))

1 lemon, preferably organic,
grated zest and juice

1 pinch freshly ground pepper,
plus extra to taste

100 g shallots, cut into halves

300 g button mushrooms,
cut into slices

50 g dry white wine

50 g cream

200 g spreadable cheese
(e.g. Laughing Cow™)
or cream cheese

2 pinches ground nutmeg

PREPARATION

1. Place water and 1 tsp salt into mixing bowl. Insert simmering basket and weigh potatoes into it. Lightly grease Varoma tray.
2. Season salmon fillets with lemon juice, remaining ½ tsp salt and pepper and place onto Varoma tray. Insert Varoma tray into Varoma dish, place Varoma into position and steam **20 min/Varoma/speed 1**. Remove Varoma, remove simmering basket with spatula, set salmon fillets and potatoes aside and keep warm. Empty mixing bowl.
3. Place shallots into mixing bowl and chop **5 sec/speed 5**. Scrape down sides of mixing bowl with spatula.
4. Add butter and sauté **2 min/120°C/speed 1**.
5. Add 150 g button mushrooms, white wine, cream and spreadable cheese and cook **5 min/90°C/speed 2**.
6. Add remaining 150 g button mushrooms, 1 heaped tsp grated lemon zest, nutmeg, salt and pepper to taste and cook **5 min/90°C/↺/speed 1**. Serve salmon with sauce and potatoes.

TIP
• When steaming in step 2 is finished, check whether potatoes are fully cooked. If not, remove Varoma with salmon and set aside to keep warm, then cook potatoes longer until tender.

VARIATION
• Serve salmon with green pasta instead of potatoes.

---

 30 min   50 min   medium   4 portions

Per portion:
Energy 2763 kJ/660 kcal
Protein 45 g/Carbs 27 g/Fat 48 g

THAI-STYLE FISH CAKES

INGREDIENTS

oil, for greasing

2-4 fresh kaffir lime leaves (see tip), stalks removed

100 g fresh green beans, trimmed

2 spring onions or shallots (approx. 40 g), cut into pieces

600 g white fish fillets (e.g. cod, snapper, perch), cut into pieces (3-4 cm)

30-50 g Thai red curry paste

60 g coconut cream or 30 g coconut cream powder diluted in 30 g warm water

1 egg white

½-1 tsp salt

1000 g water

1 long red fresh chilli, thinly sliced, to garnish

PREPARATION

1. Lightly grease Varoma dish and tray and set aside. Place kaffir lime leaves into mixing bowl and chop **10 sec/speed 10**. Scrape down sides of mixing bowl with spatula.
2. Add green beans and spring onions and chop **6-8 sec/speed 5**.
3. Place white fish fillets, Thai red curry paste, coconut cream, egg white and salt into mixing bowl and chop **Turbo/1 sec/3 times**, or until mix is well combined but not puréed.
4. Roll mixture into 18 equal-size balls (approx. 1 heaped tbsp each) and gently flatten each ball to form fish cakes. Place several fish cakes into prepared Varoma dish and tray, being careful not to let the fish cakes touch.
5. Place water into mixing bowl and place Varoma into position. Steam **16 min/Varoma/speed 2**. Transfer onto a plate and keep warm.
6. Place remaining fish cakes into Varoma dish and tray, place Varoma into position and steam **10 min/Varoma/speed 2**.
7. Serve fish cakes warm, garnished with chilli.

TIPS

- Serve fish cakes with sweet chilli dipping sauce.
- Sprinkle fish cakes with fresh coriander leaves, chopped chives or the green part of spring onions, sliced thinly.
- These fish cakes can also be pan-fried in a lightly oiled frying pan over medium-high heat.
- Rice can be steamed in the simmering basket at the same time as the fish cakes. Add 3 extra kaffir lime leaves to steaming water for extra flavour. Or steam Asian vegetables of choice alongside the fish cakes in the Varoma.
- Fresh kaffir lime leaves can be replaced with frozen kaffir lime leaves. Dried kaffir lime leaves, though less aromatic, may also be used. Or see variations for alternative flavourings.

 15 min   45 min   easy 18 18 pieces  *Per 3 pieces:*
Energy 840 kJ/202 kcal
Protein 22 g/Carbs 4 g/Fat 11 g

VARIATION
- Replace kaffir lime leaves with grated lime zest (1-2 tsp), fresh coriander leaves (5-6 sprigs, leaves only) or sliced fresh ginger (approx. 1-2 cm).

MUSSELS IN SPICY TOMATO SAUCE

INGREDIENTS

120 g onions, cut into halves

1 garlic clove

85 g olive oil

½ tsp chilli powder or dried chilli flakes, adjust to taste

1000 g fresh mussels, in the shell

200 g chopped tomatoes, fresh or canned

100 g dry white wine

1 pinch salt

PREPARATION

1. Place onions and garlic clove into mixing bowl and chop **4 sec/speed 5**. Scrape down sides of mixing bowl with spatula.
2. Add olive oil and chilli powder and sauté **7 min/120°C/speed ⚬**. Meanwhile scrub and debeard mussels (if necessary) and place them into Varoma dish. Set aside.
3. Add chopped tomatoes, wine and salt into mixing bowl, place Varoma into position and cook **13 min/Varoma/speed 1**. Remove Varoma, set aside and keep warm.
4. Reduce sauce **15 min/Varoma/speed 1**, placing simmering basket instead of measuring cup onto mixing bowl lid to help prevent splashing.
5. Transfer steamed mussels into a serving bowl, cover with sauce and serve hot.

TIPS
- Discard any mussels which are open before cooking and those that are still closed after cooking.
- Adjust quantity of olive oil to personal taste.

VARIATION
- **Vegetables in spicy tomato sauce:** As a vegetarian option make this dish with vegetables instead of mussels. Add 200 g water and some fresh herbs to the mixing bowl, then extend cooking time until vegetables are done.

 15 min 45 min easy 4 portions

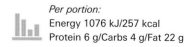
Per portion:
Energy 1076 kJ/257 kcal
Protein 6 g/Carbs 4 g/Fat 22 g

MAIN DISHES – VEGETARIAN

INDIAN VEGETABLE CURRY

INGREDIENTS

½ tsp coriander seeds

½ tsp cumin seeds

½ tsp cardamom seeds

½ tsp mustard seeds

100 g onions, cut into halves

2 garlic cloves

15 g fresh ginger, cut into thin slices

1 fresh red chilli, small, deseeded,
  cut into pieces

20 g olive oil

1 tsp ground turmeric

400 g coconut milk

100 g water

1 heaped tsp vegetable stock paste,
  homemade, or 1 vegetable
  stock cube (for 0.5 l)

2 tsp salt

600 g waxy potatoes, peeled,
  cut into pieces (2-3 cm)

150 g carrots, cut into slices (1 cm)

150 g cauliflower, cut into florets

150 g courgettes, cut into slices
  (1 cm)

100 g frozen green peas

2 sprigs fresh coriander, leaves only

PREPARATION

1. Place coriander, cumin, cardamom and mustard seeds into mixing bowl and toast **6 min/120°C/↩/speed 1**.
2. Add onions, garlic cloves, ginger and red chilli and chop **5 sec/speed 5**. Scrape down sides of mixing bowl with spatula.
3. Add olive oil and sauté **6 min/120°C/speed 1**.
4. Add turmeric, coconut milk, water, vegetable stock paste and salt and blend **1 min/speed 10**.
5. Add potatoes and carrots and cook **10 min/100°C/↩/speed ❦**. Meanwhile, insert Varoma tray into Varoma dish and place cauliflower, courgettes and frozen green peas onto Varoma tray.
6. Place Varoma into position and cook **12 min/Varoma/↩/speed 1**.
7. Remove Varoma, add vegetables from Varoma tray into mixing bowl, insert measuring cup and cook **2 min/100°C/↩/speed ❦**. Transfer curry into a bowl, garnish with coriander leaves and serve hot.

VARIATION

• Use other vegetables such as broccoli, green beans, peppers or squash.

 15 min
 50 min
 medium
 4 portions
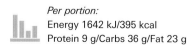
Per portion:
Energy 1642 kJ/395 kcal
Protein 9 g/Carbs 36 g/Fat 23 g

TOFU STEW

INGREDIENTS

150 g onions, cut into halves

2 garlic cloves

30 g olive oil

150 g tomatoes, fresh or canned

1 heaped tsp vegetable stock paste, homemade, or 1 vegetable stock cube (for 0.5 l)

½ tsp salt

1 pinch ground black pepper

50-100 g white wine

350 g courgettes, cut into cubes

200 g carrots, cut into slices

200 g mushrooms, cut into slices

400 g firm tofu, cut into cubes

1½ tsp dried basil

1 tsp dried oregano

PREPARATION

1. Place onions, garlic cloves, olive oil and tomatoes into mixing bowl, chop **5 sec/speed 5**, then sauté **5 min/120°C/speed 2**.
2. Add vegetable stock paste, salt, black pepper, wine, courgettes, carrots and mushrooms and sauté **12 min/Varoma/⟳/speed ⟲**.
3. Add tofu, basil and oregano and cook **4 min/100°C/⟳/speed ⟲**. Serve hot.

TIP
• Serve with rice or whole wheat pasta.

 10 min 30 min easy 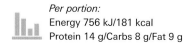 6 portions

Per portion:
Energy 756 kJ/181 kcal
Protein 14 g/Carbs 8 g/Fat 9 g

BROCCOLI AND POTATOES WITH CHEESE SAUCE

INGREDIENTS

Broccoli and potatoes
600 g broccoli, cut into florets
700 g water
½ tsp salt
500 g potatoes, cut into pieces
    (3-4 cm)

Cheese sauce
100 g blue cheese, cut into pieces
20 g flour
50 g butter
80 g cream
¼ tsp ground white pepper
1 pinch ground nutmeg

PREPARATION

Broccoli and potatoes
1. Place broccoli florets into Varoma dish and set aside. Place water and salt into mixing bowl. Insert simmering basket and weigh potatoes into it. Cook **15 min/Varoma/speed 1**.
2. Place Varoma into position and cook a further **10-15 min/Varoma/speed 1** or until broccoli is cooked as desired.
3. Remove Varoma and remove simmering basket with spatula. Transfer broccoli and potatoes into a serving dish and keep warm. Transfer cooking liquid into a bowl.

Cheese sauce
4. Place 400 g reserved cooking liquid, blue cheese, flour, butter and cream into mixing bowl and cook **10 min/90°C/speed 3**.
5. Add white pepper and nutmeg and mix **5 sec/speed 6**.
6. Pour cheese sauce over broccoli and potatoes and serve immediately.

VARIATIONS
• Replace broccoli with cauliflower.
• Add fresh dill to the sauce.

---

 15 min 45 min easy   4 portions

Per portion:
Energy 1753 kJ/418 kcal
Protein 15 g/Carbs 33 g/Fat 25 g

STUFFED VEGETABLES

INGREDIENTS

2 courgettes (130 g each)
2 aubergines (400 g each)
2 white onions (120 g each)
500 g water
10 g extra virgin olive oil, plus extra for greasing and drizzling
100 g breadcrumbs
10 fresh basil leaves
1 egg
20 g milk
½ tsp salt
1 pinch ground black pepper

USEFUL ITEMS

casserole dish

PREPARATION

1. Cut courgettes and aubergines in half lengthwise. Cut white onions in half across the middle. Arrange all vegetables in Varoma dish and tray with cut side facing down.
2. Place water into mixing bowl, place Varoma into position and steam **25 min/Varoma/speed 1**. Set Varoma aside and empty mixing bowl.
3. Preheat oven to 180°C. Grease a casserole dish and set aside.
4. Using a tablespoon, scoop out pulp of cooked vegetables, leaving the outside intact for stuffing later. Reserve pulp for use in stuffing mixture.
5. Place extra virgin olive oil, breadcrumbs, basil leaves, egg, milk, salt, black pepper and reserved pulp of cooked vegetables into mixing bowl and mix **3 sec/speed 5**.
6. Place vegetable shells cut side up into prepared casserole dish. Fill vegetable shells with stuffing mixture and drizzle with extra virgin olive oil. Bake for 20-30 min (180°C). Serve hot.

TIP
• If you don't like onions or if they are too small for stuffing, replace with 1 more aubergine or courgette or use onion for the filling only.

VARIATION
• Add 30 g grated Parmesan cheese in step 5.

Step 4   Step 6

 20 min   1 h 20 min   medium   4 portions

Per portion:
Energy 1018 kJ/243 kcal
Protein 9 g/Carbs 28 g/Fat 10 g

POTATO CAKES

INGREDIENTS

1000 g potatoes, cut into pieces
150 g onions, cut into halves
1 tbsp lemon juice
1 tsp salt
¼ tsp ground black pepper
20 g cornflour (starch)
20 g oat flakes
1 egg
frying oil

USEFUL ITEMS

non-stick frying pan
turner
paper towel

PREPARATION

1. Place potatoes, onions, lemon juice, salt, black pepper, cornflour, oat flakes and egg into mixing bowl and chop **12 sec/speed 5** with aid of spatula.
2. Pour frying oil into a hot non-stick frying pan, covering the bottom of the pan with a thin layer, and heat. Place 2 heaped tbsp of mixture per potato cake into the hot frying oil and using the spoon, flatten each heap to form a pancake shape (Ø 10 cm). Fry potato cakes on both sides until golden brown and crisp. Drain on paper towels. Serve hot.

TIPS

- Serve with apple sauce, or for a savoury alternative, with sour cream, smoked salmon or bacon.
- Use fresh potatoes. If you clean the potatoes well, there is no need to peel them.
- Depending on the kind of potatoes used, and how long the batter is left to rest before frying, you may need to add more cornflour or oat flakes, or to remove excess moisture from the batter with a spoon.
- As the batter can be prepared in seconds, it is easy to repeat this recipe quickly to increase portions for a party.

VARIATION

- **Vegetable potato cakes:** replace ⅓ of the potatoes with vegetables (e.g. carrots, kohlrabi, cauliflower, courgettes etc.) Double the amount of starch and oat flakes. Season with ground mixed pepper and serve with a sour cream and herbs dip.

Step 2

 45 min   45 min   easy   4 portions

Per portion:
Energy 1818 kJ/434 kcal
Protein 8 g/Carbs 49 g/Fat 23 g

CAULIFLOWER CHEESE

INGREDIENTS

200 g Gruyère or Cheddar cheese,
   cut into pieces
500 g water
1 cauliflower (approx. 1000 g),
   cut into florets
50 g flour
40 g butter
500 g milk
½ tsp salt, plus extra to taste
2 pinches ground white pepper,
   plus extra to taste
1-2 pinches ground nutmeg
   (optional)

USEFUL ITEMS

casserole dish

PREPARATION

1. Place Gruyère cheese into mixing bowl and grate **8 sec/speed 7**.
   Transfer into a bowl and set aside.
2. Place water into mixing bowl and cauliflower florets into Varoma dish.
   Place Varoma into position and steam **25 min/Varoma/speed 1**.
   Set Varoma aside and empty mixing bowl.
3. Place flour, butter, milk, salt and pepper into mixing bowl and cook
   7 min/90°C/speed 3.
4. Add nutmeg and 70 g reserved grated Gruyère cheese and mix
   5 sec/speed 5. Adjust seasoning to taste.
5. Preheat oven grill to 200°C.
6. Arrange cauliflower in a casserole dish, cover with sauce and sprinkle
   with remaining grated Gruyère cheese. Place under the grill for
   approx. 10 minutes (200°C) or until golden brown. Serve immediately.

VARIATION

• For a heartier dish, add hard-boiled eggs, cut into halves. Arrange them in the
   casserole dish with the cauliflower before covering with sauce. You can cook
   the eggs **15 min/Varoma/speed 1** in the simmering basket while steaming the
   cauliflower.

 10 min   50 min   easy   6
 6 portions    Per portion:
Energy 1237 kJ/305 kcal
Protein 17 g/Carbs 14 g/Fat 20 g

LENTIL MOUSSAKA

INGREDIENTS

200 g red split lentils
500 g water
120 g Parmesan cheese,
    cut into pieces
400 g aubergines
50 g olive oil
200 g onions, cut into halves
3 garlic cloves
1 pepper, green or red, cut into
    pieces (approx. 150 g)
400 g tomatoes, canned, including
    juice
120 g red wine
1 tbsp dried oregano
1 tsp ground ginger
1-2 tsp salt, to taste
½ tsp ground black pepper
40 g butter, plus extra for greasing
500 g milk
40 g flour

USEFUL ITEMS

casserole dish
    (20 cm x 30 cm x 6 cm)

PREPARATION

1. Place red split lentils and 500 g water into a bowl and soak for 1 hour.
2. Place Parmesan cheese into mixing bowl and grate **10 sec/speed 10**. Transfer into a bowl and set aside.
3. Cut aubergines into slices (1 cm thick) and place into Varoma dish. Make sure that some holes in the Varoma dish remain unobstructed so that steam passes through.
4. Place olive oil, onions, garlic cloves and green or red pepper into mixing bowl and chop **5 sec/speed 5**.
5. Add tomatoes and chop **2 sec/speed 5**.
6. Add red wine, oregano, ginger, salt and black pepper into mixing bowl. Place Varoma into position and steam **20 min/Varoma/↻/speed 1**. Set Varoma aside.
7. Add drained red lentils and cook **8 min/100°C/↻/speed 2**. Meanwhile, preheat oven to 200°C and grease a casserole dish. Arrange all aubergine slices in casserole dish and cover them with lentil mixture. No need to clean mixing bowl.
8. Place butter, milk and flour into mixing bowl and cook **8 min/90°C/speed 4**.
9. Add 60 g reserved grated Parmesan cheese to sauce and mix **5 sec/speed 4**. Cover lentil layer with sauce and sprinkle with remaining grated Parmesan cheese. Bake moussaka for 30 minutes (200°C). Cut moussaka into squares and serve hot.

TIP
• Instead of soaked red lentils you can use pre-cooked brown lentils.

 25 min   2 h 20 min   easy   6 portions   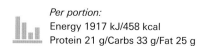 *Per portion:* Energy 1917 kJ/458 kcal Protein 21 g/Carbs 33 g/Fat 25 g

Step 7

Step 9

MAIN DISHES – OTHER

THREE COURSE MEAL FOR TWO

INGREDIENTS

Flavoured breadcrumbs

50 g bread roll or white bread
1 garlic clove
5 sprigs fresh coriander or
     fresh parsley

Three course meal

250 g carrots, cut into pieces (2-3 cm)
250 g courgettes, cut into pieces
     (2-3 cm)
100 g leek, only the white part,
     cut into slices
500 g chicken breasts, skinless,
     or turkey breasts, skinless,
     cut into strips (10 cm x 1 cm)
2 tsp salt
1 pinch ground black pepper
2 sprigs fresh thyme (optional)
1 apple, cut into eighths or pear,
     cut into eighths
1 tbsp sugar or honey
½ tsp ground cinnamon
1 lemon zest
150 g onions, cut into halves
2 garlic cloves
30 g olive oil
1 dried bay leaf
650 g water
120 g long-grain rice

Béchamel sauce

250 g milk
20 g flour
10 g butter
½ tsp salt
1 pinch ground black pepper
1 pinch ground nutmeg

PREPARATION

Flavoured breadcrumbs

1. Place bread roll, garlic clove and coriander into mixing bowl and grate **10 sec/speed 9**. Transfer into a bowl and set aside. Rinse mixing bowl.

Three course meal

2. Place 100 g carrots, 100 g courgettes and 50 g leek into mixing bowl and chop **2 sec/speed 4**. Transfer into Varoma dish.
3. Place chicken into Varoma dish on top of vegetables and season with 1 tsp salt, black pepper and thyme. Set aside.
4. Place apple, sugar, cinnamon and lemon zest on a sheet of baking paper, close parcel well and place onto Varoma tray. Set aside.
5. Place onions, garlic cloves and olive oil into mixing bowl and chop **5 sec/speed 5**.
6. Add bay leaf and sauté **5 min/120°C/↻/speed ❅**.
7. Remove bay leaf, add remaining 150 g carrots, remaining 150 g courgettes, remaining 50 g leek, water and 1 tsp salt. Insert simmering basket, weigh rice into it and mix well with spatula to wet all rice grains. Insert Varoma tray into Varoma dish, place Varoma into position and cook **20 min/Varoma/speed 1**. Remove Varoma and remove simmering basket with spatula and set aside. Keep rice warm until ready to serve.
8. Insert measuring cup and blend **1 min/speed 5-9, increasing speed gradually**. Transfer vegetable soup into a bowl and keep warm.

Continued on page **192** ▶

 20 min   1 h 15 min   medium   2 portions

Per portion:
Energy 4222 kJ/1010 kcal
Protein 78 g/Carbs 109 g/Fat 28 g

▶ Three course meal for two, continued

Béchamel sauce

9. Preheat oven to 180°C.
10. Place milk, flour, butter, salt, black pepper and nutmeg into mixing bowl and cook **5 min/90°C/speed 4**. Place chicken with reserved vegetables into a casserole dish, cover with béchamel sauce and sprinkle with reserved flavoured breadcrumbs. Bake for approx. 20 minutes (180°C) or until brown. Serve vegetable soup as a starter, followed by baked chicken and vegetables casserole with rice and finish with steamed apple for dessert.

TIP
• Steamed apple can be served with vanilla or any other flavour of ice cream.

VARIATIONS
• Courgettes, carrots and leek can be replaced with the same weight of other vegetables, such as broccoli.
• Replace chicken breasts with white fish fillets.

Step 7

CREAMY VEGETABLE SOUP, STEAMED CHICKEN WITH VEGETABLE TAGLIATELLE AND MUSTARD SAUCE

INGREDIENTS

**Soup, steamed chicken and
vegetable tagliatelle**

80-100 g onions, cut into halves
1 garlic clove
20 g olive oil
1-2 carrots, for vegetable tagliatelle
1 courgette, for vegetable tagliatelle
400 g water
2 level tsp salt
450 g mixed vegetables
    (e.g. potato, courgette, carrots,
    leek), cut into pieces
500 g chicken breast fillets,
    cut into strips (5 cm x 2 cm),
    or 500 g turkey breast fillets,
    cut into strips (5 cm x 2 cm)
20 g butter or 1 tbsp cream
    (optional)

Sauce

50 g crème fraîche or 50 g cream,
    min. 30% fat
1 tbsp mustard
½ tsp salt
1 pinch ground black pepper
3-4 sprigs fresh parsley, leaves only
1 egg yolk (optional)

PREPARATION

Soup, steamed chicken and vegetable tagliatelle

1. Place onions, garlic clove and olive oil into mixing bowl and chop **5 sec/speed 5**. Scrape down sides of mixing bowl with spatula.

2. Use a vegetable peeler to cut carrots and courgette into long thin strips similar to tagliatelle pasta, stopping before you reach the core of the carrots or the seeds in the courgette. Place carrot and courgette tagliatelle loosely into Varoma dish and set aside. Cut remaining carrot and courgette cores into pieces and place into mixing bowl. Add olive oil and heat **1 min 30 sec/80°C/speed 1**, without measuring cup.

3. Add water and salt. Place mixed vegetables in simmering basket and insert into mixing bowl. Place chicken on Varoma tray, insert into Varoma and place Varoma into position. Steam **20 min/Varoma/⌇/speed ⬕**.

4. Remove Varoma and keep warm. Remove simmering basket using spatula and transfer contents into mixing bowl. Add butter and blend **1 min/speed 10**.

5. Add water until the 1 or 1.5 litre mark (depending on type of vegetables and desired soup consistency), and mix **10 sec/speed 5**.

Continued on page **194** ▶

 20 min 45 min easy 4 portions

per portions:
Energy 1973 kJ/473 kcal
Protein 34 g/Carbs 20 g/Fat 29 g

▶ Creamy vegetable soup, steamed chicken with vegetable tagliatelle and mustard sauce, continued

Sauce

6. To make the sauce, transfer almost all the soup into a serving bowl, keeping enough soup in the mixing bowl to cover the lowest blade of the mixing knife. Add crème fraîche, mustard, salt, pepper, parsley and egg yolk and mix **20 sec/speed 7**, then heat **2 min/60°C/speed 2**.

Serving

7. Serve creamy vegetable soup hot or allow to cool, cover and refrigerate for later use. Transfer chicken to a serving dish, arrange vegetable tagliatelle around the chicken and serve hot with sauce.

VARIATIONS
- In step 2, replace olive oil with 20 g butter.
- Replace chicken fillets with fish fillets (1.5 cm thick). For the sauce, replace mustard with freshly squeezed juice from half a lemon and add a pinch of cumin (optional).
- Vary or add vegetables according to the season and your preferences. For instance, add broccoli florets or turnips, cut into pieces, to the Varoma and steam together with the vegetable tagliatelle.

Step 3

SIDE DISHES

TOMATO RICE

INGREDIENTS

150 g onions, cut into halves

2 garlic cloves

200 g fresh tomatoes, cut into
   halves, or canned tomatoes

50 g olive oil

400 g long-grain rice (not parboiled)

2 tsp salt

1200 g water

PREPARATION

1. Place onions, garlic cloves, tomatoes and olive oil into mixing bowl, chop **5 sec/speed 5**, then sauté **5 min/120°C/speed 1**.
2. Add rice, salt and water, mix well with spatula and cook **17 min/100°C/☁/speed 1**. Serve immediately.

TIPS

• Serve as a side dish for fish, meat or poultry.
• This dish has a fairly liquid consistency.

VARIATION

• In step 2 add 50 g sun-dried tomatoes, cut into small cubes.

 10 min   30 min   easy   8 portions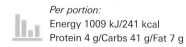

Per portion:
Energy 1009 kJ/241 kcal
Protein 4 g/Carbs 41 g/Fat 7 g

MASHED POTATOES

INGREDIENTS

1000 g floury potatoes, peeled,
    cut into slices (0.5 cm, see tip)
1 tsp salt
350 g milk
30 g butter, cut into pieces
1-2 pinches ground nutmeg

PREPARATION

1. **Insert butterfly whisk.** Place potatoes, salt and milk into mixing bowl and cook without measuring cup **25-30 min/98°C/speed 1.** If milk boils into mixing bowl lid, reduce temperature to 95°C.

2. Add butter and nutmeg, insert measuring cup and mash **30 sec/speed 3**. Serve hot.

TIPS

• The best potato purée is achieved using floury potatoes.
• Depending on the variety of potatoes used, it may be necessary to extend cooking time up to 5 minutes.

VARIATIONS

• If you prefer a more liquid purée, add 100 g milk in step 2.
• **Italian-style potato purée:** prepare the potato purée using only ½ tsp salt in step 1, and add 30 g grated Parmesan cheese in step 2.

 15 min   45 min   easy   4 portions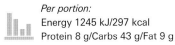

Per portion:
Energy 1245 kJ/297 kcal
Protein 8 g/Carbs 43 g/Fat 9 g

POTATO AND VEGETABLE PURÉE

INGREDIENTS

600 g floury potatoes, peeled,
    cut into slices (0.5 cm)
400 g vegetables
    (e.g. pumpkin, carrots, celeriac,
    yams, peas, cauliflower,
    broccoli), cut into slices (0.5 cm)
    as needed (see tip)
1-1¼ tsp salt
350 g milk
30 g butter
1 pinch ground nutmeg

PREPARATION

1. **Insert butterfly whisk.** Place potatoes, vegetables, salt, milk and butter into mixing bowl and cook **25-30 min/98°C/speed 1**, placing simmering basket instead of measuring cup onto mixing bowl lid to help prevent splashing.
2. **Remove butterfly whisk.** Add nutmeg, insert measuring cup and mash **30 sec/speed 4**. Serve hot.

TIPS

- If you choose vegetables with a high water content, such as courgettes, tomatoes or cucumbers, reduce milk to 300 g.
- If you choose vegetables that require a long cooking time, such as carrots, cut them into thinner slices or extend cooking time by a few minutes until vegetables are tender.

 15 min
 40 min
 easy
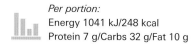 4 portions

Per portion:
Energy 1041 kJ/248 kcal
Protein 7 g/Carbs 32 g/Fat 10 g

RATATOUILLE

INGREDIENTS

120 g onions, cut into halves

2 garlic cloves

20 g olive oil

300 g ripe tomatoes,
    cut into pieces (2-3 cm)

100 g red peppers,
    cut into pieces (2-3 cm)

1 tbsp mixed dried herbs
    (e. g. thyme, rosemary,
    marjoram, basil, parsley)

1 tsp salt

2 pinches freshly ground
    black pepper

300 g aubergines,
    cut into pieces (2-3 cm)

200 g courgettes,
    cut into pieces (2-3 cm)

PREPARATION

1. Place onions, garlic cloves and olive oil into mixing bowl and chop **4 sec/speed 5**. Scrape down sides of mixing bowl with spatula.
2. Sauté **5 min/120°C/↻/speed ◑**.
3. Add tomatoes, red peppers, mixed dried herbs, salt and black pepper and cook **12 min/100°C/↻/speed ◑**.
4. Add aubergines and courgettes and cook a further **12 min/100°C/↻/speed ◑**. Serve hot or cold as a side dish.

TIPS
- Serve with roasted meat or fish, or with pasta as a vegetarian main dish.
- Sprinkle ratatouille with grated Parmesan cheese.

VARIATION
- Replace dried herbs with fresh herbs. Use sparingly and taste ratatouille before adding more.

 15 min   40 min   easy   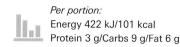 4 portions

Per portion:
Energy 422 kJ/101 kcal
Protein 3 g/Carbs 9 g/Fat 6 g

STEAMED CARROT AND COURGETTE TAGLIATELLE

INGREDIENTS

400 g carrots
400 g courgettes, small, unpeeled
500 g water
1½ tbsp extra virgin olive oil
1 tbsp lemon juice
salt, to taste

USEFUL ITEMS

vegetable peeler

PREPARATION

1. Use a vegetable peeler to cut carrots into long thin slices. Cut each slice lengthwise into strips (1 cm) similar to tagliatelle pasta. Repeat with courgettes. If necessary deseed courgettes with a spoon and then slice courgettes lengthwise with vegetable peeler in such a way that some green peel remains on each strip. Place carrot and courgette tagliatelle loosely into Varoma dish.
2. Place water into mixing bowl, place Varoma into position and steam **18 min/Varoma/speed 1**. Place steamed vegetables into a serving bowl and season with extra virgin olive oil, lemon juice and salt. Serve hot.

VARIATION
• Serve vegetable tagliatelle with tomato sauce.

Tip

 15 min 35 min medium 6 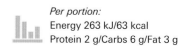 6 portions

Per portion:
Energy 263 kJ/63 kcal
Protein 2 g/Carbs 6 g/Fat 3 g

STIR-FRIED VEGETABLES

INGREDIENTS

10 g garlic cloves

10 g extra virgin olive oil

300 g pak choi, or other green
vegetable, cut into strips
(see tip)

½ tsp salt

1 pinch ground black pepper

PREPARATION

1. Place garlic cloves and extra virgin olive oil into mixing bowl and chop **3 sec/speed 5**. Scrape down sides of mixing bowl with spatula.
2. Sauté **2 min/120°C/speed ⚬**.
3. Add pak choi, salt and black pepper and stir-fry **5 min/120°C/⟲/speed ⚬**. Serve immediately.

TIPS

- Cut thick white parts of pak choi into smaller pieces (5 cm) and green leafy parts into larger pieces (10-15 cm).
- Different kinds of vegetables will require different cooking times. If vegetables seem undercooked, or if you like your vegetables softer, stir-fry a further **2-3 min/120°C/⟲/speed ⚬**.

VARIATIONS

- Replace pak choi with spinach (including stalks), water spinach or Chinese broccoli.
- In step 2 add carrot strips to give colour to the dish.

Tip

 10 min 10 min easy 4  4 portions

Per portion:
Energy 151 kJ/36 kcal
Protein 1 g/Carbs 2 g/Fat 3 g

BAKING – SAVOURY

CHEESE CRACKERS

INGREDIENTS

200 g Edam cheese, cut into pieces
    or Gruyère cheese, cut into
    pieces
200 g flour
120 g butter, unsalted, chilled,
    cut into pieces
1 egg
½-1 tsp salt
cumin seeds, for sprinkling
    (optional)
sesame seeds, for sprinkling
    (optional)

USEFUL ITEMS

cling film
baking tray and paper
cooling rack
air-tight container

PREPARATION

1. Place cheese into mixing bowl and grate **10 sec/speed 7**.
2. Add flour, butter, egg and salt and mix **30 sec/speed 4**.
3. Remove dough from mixing bowl, place on a long sheet of cling film and shape a thin log (approx. 40 cm long, Ø 4 cm). Wrap log in cling film and refrigerate until firm enough to cut into slices (approx. 2 hours).
4. Preheat oven to 180°C. Line a baking tray with baking paper and set aside.
5. Cut dough log into thin slices (3 mm thick), place slices onto prepared baking tray, sprinkle with cumin and/or sesame seeds and bake for 10-15 minutes (180°C) until golden brown. Allow to cool on a cooling rack before serving or storing in an air-tight container.

TIPS

• Serve cheese crackers with beer or wine.
• The cheese cracker dough can be prepared a day or two in advance, or frozen for several weeks, and sliced and baked shortly before serving.

VARIATIONS

• Replace Edam cheese with any strong-flavoured hard or semi-hard cheese (e.g. Cheddar).
• Omit salt in dough, and sprinkle with coarse salt before baking.
• Instead of 200 g cheese, grate a total of 250 g cheese and reserve 50 g for sprinkling on crackers before baking.
• **Cheese straws:** Instead of shaping dough into a log for slicing, form into a flattened ball and wrap in cling film. Refrigerate for 1 hour, then roll out dough (3 mm thick) between 2 sheets of baking paper and cut strips (approx. 10 cm x 1.5 cm) with a fluted pastry wheel. Bake as directed by the recipe.

 15 min
 2 h 30 min
 easy
60
60 pieces
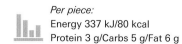
Per piece:
Energy 337 kJ/80 kcal
Protein 3 g/Carbs 5 g/Fat 6 g

Step 5

MUSHROOM PIE

INGREDIENTS

400 g puff pastry
4 garlic cloves
10 g oil
300 g water
750 g fresh button mushrooms,
  cut into slices
2 tsp mixed herbes de Provence or
  mixed dried herbs
½ tsp salt, adjust to taste
¼ tsp ground black pepper,
  adjust to taste
2 eggs
20 g flour or cornflour (starch)
50 g crème fraîche or mascarpone
10 g milk, for glazing

USEFUL ITEMS

tart tin (Ø 26 cm)
baking paper
rolling pin
pastry brush

PREPARATION

1. Divide puff pastry into 2 equal pieces and refrigerate until needed.
2. Place garlic cloves and oil into mixing bowl and chop **3 sec/speed 5**. Scrape down sides of mixing bowl with spatula
3. Cook **7 min/100°C/speed ∿**. Transfer into a bowl and set aside.
4. Place water into mixing bowl. Place button mushrooms into Varoma, sprinkle with herbs, salt and black pepper. Place Varoma into position and steam **10 min/Varoma/speed 2**.
5. Stir mushrooms with spatula to ensure even cooking. Steam a further **10 min/Varoma/speed 2**. Remove Varoma and set aside. Empty mixing bowl.
6. Preheat oven to 200°C. Line the base of a tart tin (Ø 26 cm) with baking paper and set aside.
7. Using a rolling pin, roll out one piece of pastry on a lightly floured surface. Line prepared tart tin with the pastry and set aside. Roll out the second piece of pastry and gently score its surface with the point of a sharp knife, making a criss-cross pattern without cutting through the dough. In the centre of the pastry, cut a cross and fold back its corners to create a small opening. Set aside. Spread mushrooms into pastry-lined tart tin.
8. Place reserved cooked garlic, eggs, flour and crème fraîche into mixing bowl and cook **5 min/80°C/speed 2**, then blend **10 sec/speed 6**.
9. Pour sauce over mushrooms, cover pie with second pastry disk, seal well around the edges, brush pie surface with milk and bake 30-35 minutes (200°C), or until golden brown. Serve hot or warm.

VARIATION
• Combine button mushrooms with other mushroom varieties (e.g. porcini, chanterelles, crimini, portobello, morels, shiitake).

---

 25 min   1 h 30 min   medium   6 portions    *Per portion:* Energy 1476 kJ/353 kcal Protein 12 g/Carbs 28 g/Fat 22 g

Step 7

Step 9

PIZZA MARGHERITA

INGREDIENTS

Pizza dough

30 g extra virgin olive oil,
 plus extra for greasing
220 g water, room temperature
1 tsp sugar or malt powder
20 g fresh yeast, crumbled,
 or 2 tsp dried instant yeast (8 g)
400 g bread flour, plus extra for
 dusting
1 tsp salt

Margherita topping

200 g mozzarella, cut into pieces
250 g chopped tomatoes, canned
2-3 pinches salt, to taste
1 tbsp extra virgin olive oil
10-15 fresh basil leaves, torn into
 pieces

USEFUL ITEMS

cling film or kitchen towel
baking tray (approx. 40 cm x 35 cm)
baking paper

PREPARATION

Pizza dough

1. Lightly grease a large bowl and set aside. Place water, sugar and yeast into mixing bowl and mix **20 sec/speed 2**.
2. Add bread flour, extra virgin olive oil and salt and knead **2 min/🌾**. Place dough into prepared bowl and form into a ball. Cover bowl with cling film or a damp kitchen towel and let dough rise until doubled in size (approx. 1 hour).

Margherita topping

3. Preheat oven to 230°C. Line a baking tray (approx. 40 cm x 35 cm) with baking paper or grease with extra virgin olive oil and set aside.
4. Place mozzarella into mixing bowl and chop **3 sec/speed 5**. Transfer into simmering basket and leave to drain for 10 minutes.
5. Place dough on prepared baking tray and shape into a rectangle the size of the baking tray by pressing it with your finger tips and stretching it gently. Form a small ridge around the edges.
6. Spread chopped tomatoes and mozzarella on top of dough and sprinkle with salt, olive oil and 5-7 torn basil leaves. Bake pizza for 20 minutes (230°C). Scatter additional 5-8 torn basil leaves (to taste) over pizza and serve hot.

TIPS
- Alternatively, roll pizza dough out on a floured surface using a rolling pin, and transfer dough onto prepared baking tray.
- 4 individual round pizzas can be made from the dough. Bake them one at a time and share each pizza as it comes fresh out of the oven.
- In step 2, lightly oil the cling film to avoid sticking.
- If the mozzarella is dry there is no need to drain it.
- If the chopped tomatoes have a lot of liquid, drain through simmering basket.

VARIATION
- Add your favourite toppings (e.g. vegetables, salami, ham, cheese, fruit, herbs).

Step 6

 25 min 2 h 10 min easy 4 4 portions

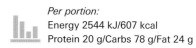 *Per portion:*
Energy 2544 kJ/607 kcal
Protein 20 g/Carbs 78 g/Fat 24 g

QUICHE LORRAINE

INGREDIENTS

50 g Gruyère cheese,
    cut into pieces (optional)

Pastry

75 g butter, unsalted, cut into
    pieces, plus extra for greasing
150 g flour, plus extra for dusting
½ tsp salt
50 g water

Filling

200 g bacon cubes
4 eggs
50 g milk
100 g crème fraîche or cream
¼ tsp salt
2 pinches ground black pepper

USEFUL ITEMS

quiche tin (Ø 26 cm)
rolling pin

PREPARATION

1. Place Gruyère cheese into mixing bowl and grate **10 sec/speed 7**. Transfer into a bowl and set aside.

Pastry

2. Preheat oven to 180°C. Grease and flour a quiche tin (Ø 26 cm) and set aside.
3. Place flour, butter, salt and water into mixing bowl and mix **20 sec/speed 4**. Remove pastry from mixing bowl and form into a ball.
4. Using a rolling pin, roll out pastry on a lightly floured surface. Line prepared quiche tin with the pastry, prick with a fork to avoid air bubbles and set aside.

Filling

5. Place bacon cubes into mixing bowl and sauté **3 min/120°C/speed ꙮ**. Drain bacon through simmering basket and discard fat. Set bacon aside.
6. Place eggs, milk, crème fraîche, salt and black pepper into mixing bowl and mix **30 sec/speed 4**.
7. Distribute reserved sautéed bacon cubes onto pastry and cover with egg mixture. Sprinkle reserved grated Gruyère cheese and bake for 25 minutes (180°C) or until golden. Serve warm or cold.

TIPS
- Serve with a mixed salad for a main course.
- Bacon is salty, therefore use salt sparingly or to your taste.

VARIATION
- **Vegetarian quiche:** instead of bacon cubes, use sun-dried tomatoes preserved in oil. Omit step 5, drain tomatoes and cut into small cubes before placing onto pastry in step 7. Proceed as directed by the recipe.

Step 4

 20 min   45 min   medium   8 8 slices

Per slice:
Energy 1215 kJ/290 kcal
Protein 13 g/Carbs 17 g/Fat 19 g

BREADS AND ROLLS

SANDWICH BREAD

INGREDIENTS

30 g butter, plus extra for greasing
240 g water
1 tsp dried instant yeast (4 g)
    or 10 g fresh yeast
30 g brown sugar
500 g bread flour
1 tsp salt

USEFUL ITEMS

loaf tin (30 cm x 12 cm x 10 cm)
kitchen towel
cooling rack

PREPARATION

1. Grease a loaf tin (approx. 30 cm x 12 cm x 10 cm) and set aside.
2. Place water, dried yeast, brown sugar and butter into mixing bowl and mix **1 min/37°C/speed 2**.
3. Add flour and salt and knead **3 min/**. Transfer dough into a large bowl, cover with a damp kitchen towel and let rise in a warm place until doubled in size (approx. 1 hour). Divide dough into 3 parts, form each into a ball and place them into prepared loaf tin. Cover with damp kitchen towel and let rise again in a warm place until doubled in size (approx. 1 hour). Meanwhile, preheat oven to 180°C.
4. Bake for 30 minutes (180°C). Remove loaf from tin and allow to cool on a cooling rack before slicing.

TIPS
• Enjoy fresh or toasted with butter and jam or another spread.
• For a nice colour brush with milk before baking.

VARIATION
• **Wholemeal sandwich bread:** Before starting the recipe, place 250 g wheat grains into mixing bowl and grind **1 min/speed 10**. Transfer into a bowl and proceed with the recipe, using only 250 g bread flour plus the reserved ground wheat flour, and a total of 270 g water instead of 240 g.

Step 3

 10 min   3 h   easy   24
 24 slices   *Per slice:*
Energy 375 kJ/90 kcal
Protein 2 g/Carbs 16 g/Fat 2 g

FOCACCIA WITH ONIONS

INGREDIENTS

Dough

20 g olive oil, plus extra for
   greasing
600 g bread flour
30 g fresh yeast, crumbled or
   3 tsp dried instant yeast (12 g)
380 g water
1 pinch sugar
1 tsp salt

Topping

40 g extra virgin olive oil
40 g water
1½ tsp salt
400 g onions, cut into halves

USEFUL ITEMS

baking tray (approx. 40 cm x 35 cm)
baking paper
large bowl or cling film

PREPARATION

Dough

1. Line a baking tray (approx. 40 cm x 35 cm) with baking paper and grease the baking paper with 2 tbsp olive oil. Set aside.
2. Place flour, fresh yeast, water, 20 g olive oil, sugar and salt into mixing bowl and knead **3 min/**.
3. With aid of oiled spatula transfer dough onto prepared baking tray. With oiled hands, form dough into a round shape and cover with a thin coating of olive oil. Cover dough with a large bowl or cling film and let rise in a warm place until doubled in size (approx. 1 hour). Meanwhile preheat oven to 220°C.
4. Without kneading the dough any further, spread it out with oiled finger tips into a rectangle the size of the baking tray and set tray aside.

Topping

5. Place olive oil, water and salt into mixing bowl and emulsify **10 sec/speed 4**.
6. Add onions into mixing bowl, chop **6 sec/speed 4** and spread on top of dough. Bake for 20-25 minutes (220°C) or until golden brown. Cool before cutting into squares and serving.

TIPS
- Focaccia can be served with meals or as a sandwich bread.
- The dough is quite wet but keeping its surface well oiled prevents it from sticking to fingers.
- Use scissors to cut focaccia into squares.

VARIATION
- **Plain focaccia with salt:** omit onions in step 5 and brush oil, water and salt emulsion from step 4 directly over the surface of the dough. Sprinkle with 1 tsp coarse salt and bake as directed by the recipe.

 10 min   1 h 30 min   medium   16 pieces  *Per piece:* Energy 797 kJ/190 kcal Protein 5 g/Carbs 28 g/Fat 6 g

Step 4

RUSTIC BREAD

INGREDIENTS

600 g wheat grains
400 g water
30 g fresh yeast or
    3 tsp dried instant yeast (12 g)
120 g buttermilk
150 g bread flour,
    plus extra for dusting
2 tsp salt
1 tbsp balsamic vinegar
1 tsp malt powder (optional)

USEFUL ITEMS

baking tray and paper
cooling rack

PREPARATION

1. Place 200 g wheat grains into mixing bowl and grind **1 min/speed 10**. Transfer into a large bowl.
2. Again place 200 g wheat grains into mixing bowl and grind **1 min/speed 10**. Transfer into the large bowl.
3. Again place remaining 200 g wheat grains into mixing bowl, grind **1 min/speed 10**, transfer into the large bowl and set aside.
4. Place water, yeast and buttermilk into mixing bowl and warm **2 min/37°C/speed 2**.
5. Add reserved ground wheat grains, bread flour, salt, balsamic vinegar and malt powder. Knead **3 min/🌾** then let rise in mixing bowl with lid on until dough rises to top of bowl (approx. 30 minutes).
6. Knead a further **1 min/🌾**.
7. Preheat oven to 220°C. Line a baking tray with baking paper and set aside.
8. Turn dough out onto a floured surface. Using floured hands, shape dough into a loaf, place onto prepared baking tray and let rise again while oven is heating (approx. 15 minutes). Using a sharp knife, slash top of loaf in a criss-cross pattern and bake for 15 minutes (220°C).
9. Reduce temperature to 190°C and bake for a further 20-25 minutes or until loaf sounds hollow when tapped on the underside. Allow to cool on a cooling rack before slicing.

TIPS

- If some of the dough sticks to the mixing knife blades when transferring it to the floured surface in step 8, place mixing bowl back into position and mix **2 sec/speed 10**. The remaining dough should now be easy to remove using the spatula.
- You can let the loaf rise in a rising basket and then tip it onto the baking tray just before baking. This will help the loaf retain its shape while rising.

 20 min   2 h   medium   35 35 slices   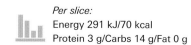 Per slice:
Energy 291 kJ/70 kcal
Protein 3 g/Carbs 14 g/Fat 0 g

VARIATIONS

- Replace buttermilk with yoghurt or with milk to which 1 tsp of vinegar has been added, or with sour cream.
- Replace wheat grains with spelt grains, or 100 g of the wheat grains with 100 g rye grains.
- Bake the bread in a loaf tin. After baking, remove loaf from tin and allow to cool on a cooling rack.

Step 6

FIVE SEED BREAD

INGREDIENTS

500 g water

2 tsp dried instant yeast or
     20 g fresh yeast

30 g extra virgin olive oil,
     plus extra for greasing

500 g bread flour

1 tsp salt

50 g rolled oats

30 g sesame seeds,
     plus extra for sprinkling

30 g linseeds, plus extra for
     sprinkling

30 g sunflower seeds,
     plus extra for sprinkling

30 g pumpkin seeds,
     plus extra for sprinkling

30 g poppy seeds,
     plus extra for sprinkling

30 g honey

USEFUL ITEMS

loaf tin (30 cm x 12 cm x 10 cm)
cooling rack

PREPARATION

1. Place water and yeast into mixing bowl and warm
   2 min 30 sec/37°C/speed 2. Meanwhile, grease a loaf tin
   (approx. 30 cm x 12 cm x 10 cm) and set aside.

2. Add bread flour, salt, rolled oats, sesame seeds, linseeds, sunflower
   seeds, pumpkin seeds, poppy seeds, honey and extra virgin olive oil
   into mixing bowl and knead **2 min 30 sec/⚕**. Dough will have a wet
   and sticky consistency (see tip).

3. Transfer dough into prepared loaf tin and sprinkle with extra sesame
   seeds, linseeds, sunflower seeds, pumpkin seeds, and poppy
   seeds. Let rise uncovered in a warm place until doubled in size
   (approx. 45-60 minutes). Meanwhile, preheat oven to 200°C.

4. Bake for 40-45 minutes (200°C). Allow to cool in tin 5 minutes.
   Transfer to a cooling rack and allow to cool before slicing.

TIP

• This dough is very sticky, but there is no need to add more flour as the wet dough
  produces a crunchy crust and moist crumb.

 10 min   1 h 50 min   easy   20 slices

Per slice:
Energy 1289 kJ/308 kcal
Protein 10 g/Carbs 36 g/Fat 13 g

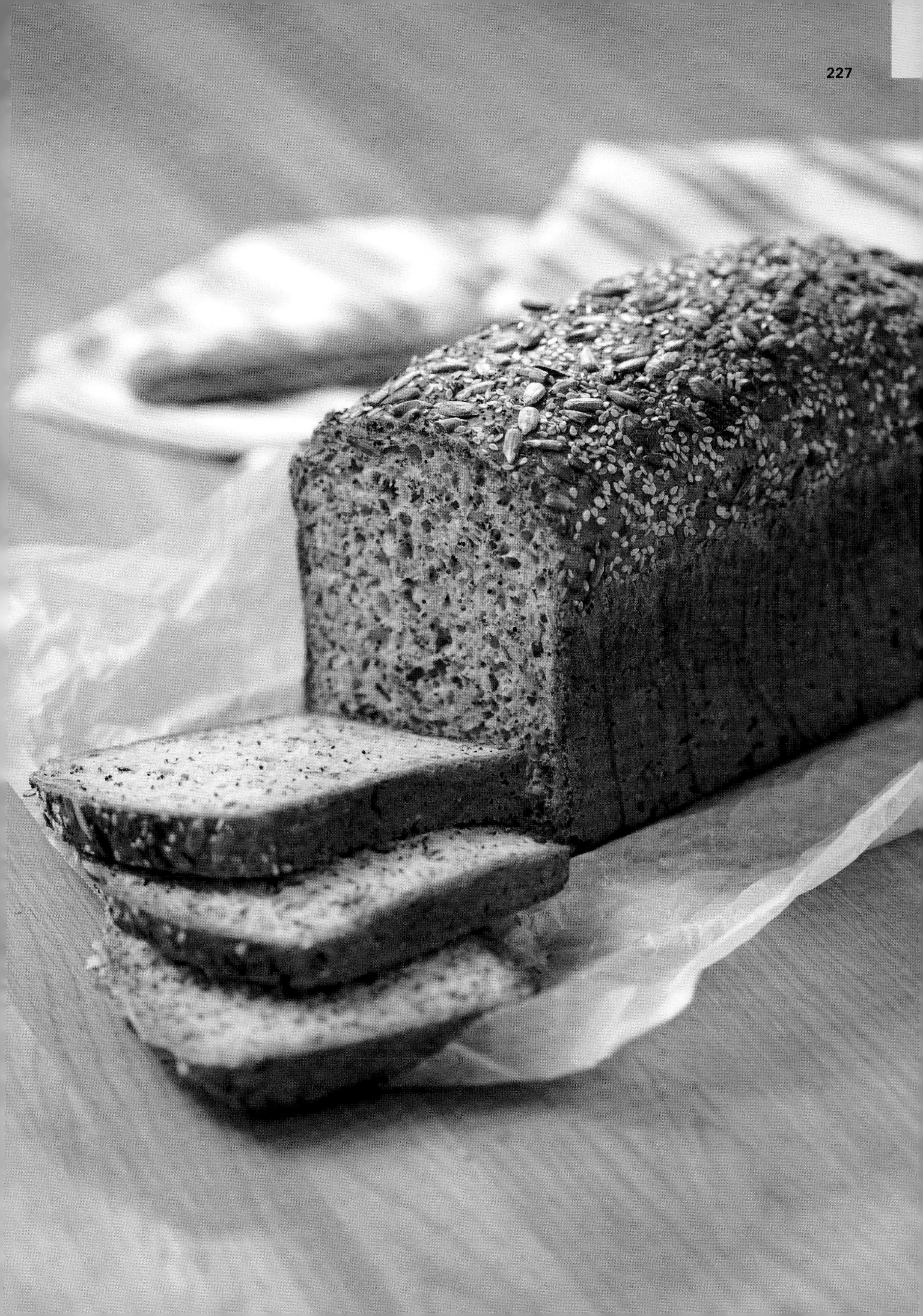

SPELT BREAD

INGREDIENTS

700 g spelt grains
550 g water, lukewarm
40 g fresh yeast, crumbled or
    4 tsp dried instant yeast (16 g)
2 tsp sugar
100 g sunflower seeds
1 pinch ground allspice
¼ tsp ground coriander
2 tsp salt

USEFUL ITEMS

loaf tin (30 cm x 12 cm x 10 cm)
baking paper
cooling rack

PREPARATION

1. Place 250 g spelt grains into mixing bowl and grind **1 min/speed 10**. Transfer into a bowl and set aside.
2. Place 450 g spelt grains into mixing bowl and grind coarsely **1 min/speed 10**.
3. Add water, reserved ground spelt grains, fresh yeast, sugar, sunflower seeds, allspice, coriander and salt and knead **5 min/**.
4. Preheat oven to 250°C. Line a loaf tin (30 x 12 cm x 10 cm) with baking paper or grease it lightly.
5. Place dough into prepared loaf tin and let rise in a warm place for 15 minutes.
6. Bake for 20 minutes (250°C) then reduce oven temperature to 200°C and bake for a further 30 minutes more (200°C). Remove loaf from tin and allow to cool on a cooling rack before slicing.

TIPS

- The recipe works well with only 15 minutes rising in step 5. If you wish, you can decrease the yeast amount and increase the rising time.
- If the crust browns too quickly, cover bread with aluminium foil towards the end of the baking time.
- The bread is ready when it sounds hollow if you tap its underside.

 10 min   1 h 45 min   easy   30 / 30 slices

Per slice:
Energy 406 kJ/97 kcal
Protein 4 g/Carbs 16 g/Fat 2 g

PITTA BREAD

INGREDIENTS

1 tsp dried instant yeast (4 g)
    or 10 g fresh yeast
270 g water
1 tsp sugar
1 tsp olive oil
500 g bread flour
1 tsp salt

USEFUL ITEMS

cling film
rolling pin
baking tray
kitchen towel

PREPARATION

1. Place dried yeast, water and sugar into mixing bowl and warm **30 sec/37°C/speed 2**.
2. Add olive oil, bread flour and salt and knead **3 min/ᘉ**. Transfer dough into a bowl, cover with cling film and let rise in a warm place until doubled in size (approx. 1 h). Divide dough into 7-8 pieces, form each into a ball and allow to rest for 15 minutes. With a rolling pin roll each ball into a flat circle (approx. Ø 15 cm) and allow to rest for a further 15 minutes.
3. Meanwhile, preheat oven and baking tray to 250°C.
4. Place 2-4 dough circles onto preheated baking tray and bake for 4-5 minutes (250°C) until puffed up or pale golden. Repeat with remaining dough. Transfer hot pitta breads onto a plate and cover immediately with a dry kitchen towel to keep them soft. Allow to cool before serving.

TIPS

- Cut pitta bread in half to fill with sandwich fillings (e.g. lettuce leaves, tomatoes, cheese, cold meat, mayonnaise).
- Placing dough on preheated baking tray helps it puff up. If a few of the pitta breads don't puff up, they can still be served as soft flat breads.

Step 2   Step 4

 15 min   2 h   medium   8 pieces

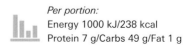

Per portion:
Energy 1000 kJ/238 kcal
Protein 7 g/Carbs 49 g/Fat 1 g

BAGUETTE

INGREDIENTS

330 g water
10 g fresh yeast, crumbled or
    1 tsp dried instant yeast (4 g)
oil, for greasing
500 g bread flour, plus extra
    for dusting
1½ tsp salt

USEFUL ITEMS

cling film or kitchen towel
    (tea towel)
baking paper
2 baking trays
    (approx. 40 cm x 35 cm)

PREPARATION

1. Place water and yeast into mixing bowl and warm
   2 min/37°C/speed 2. Meanwhile, lightly grease a large bowl and
   set aside.
2. Add flour and salt and knead **2 min/ᵞ**. Transfer dough into prepared
   bowl. Cover bowl with cling film or a damp kitchen towel (tea towel)
   and let rise until doubled in size (approx. 1½ hours).
3. On a lightly floured surface, use a large knife to separate dough into
   three equal pieces. Gently flatten and roll each piece loosely into a log
   shape and set aside on a lightly floured surface. Dust rolls lightly with
   flour, cover with cling film or a damp kitchen towel and allow to rest
   for 20 minutes.
4. Again, gently flatten each piece of dough into a rectangle, taking care
   to preserve the air bubbles trapped within. Roll dough again into a log
   shape. Pinch seam of roll with your fingers to seal. Elongate roll into
   a baguette shape, rolling back and forth exerting gentle pressure from
   the middle of the baguette to its ends. Place baguettes seam-side
   down onto baking paper, pulling up paper between baguettes to create
   a low wall. This will help baguettes to hold their shape and will
   prevent them from sticking to each other as they rise. Cover baguettes
   loosely with cling film or a damp kitchen towel and let rise for a
   further 45 minutes.
5. 20 minutes before end of rising time, place 2 baking trays into lower
   part of oven, one tray on the lowest rung, the other on a rung above.
   Preheat oven to 250°C.

Continued on page **234** ▶

 30 min   3 h 45 min   advanced   30  30 slices

Per piece:
Energy 2531 kJ/604 kcal
Protein 19 g/Carbs 122 g/Fat 4 g

▶ Baguette, continued

6. Prepare approx. 100 g very hot water in a cup. Slash baguettes with a very sharp knife, making three overlapping slashes along the length of each bread. Slide baguettes, together with baking paper, onto the top preheated baking tray. Quickly but also **carefully** splash the hot water onto the lower baking tray to create steam (see tip) and immediately close oven door to trap the steam. Bake for 20 minutes (250°C), or until dark golden brown. If baguettes seem quite brown before end of baking time, reduce oven temperature to 230°C. Allow baguettes to cool for 20 minutes before slicing.

TIPS
- To test if baguettes are ready to bake, gently press dough with your fingertip. The indentation left by your finger should slowly disappear. If the dough springs up quickly then it has not risen sufficiently. If the indentation remains, the dough has over-proved. The baguettes won't rise as much in the oven but they will still taste good.
- Creating the burst of steam at the beginning of baking gives the baguettes their crisp, golden crust. Be very careful not to splash yourself or any glass elements in your oven. You may omit the steam if desired.
- Baguettes are always best eaten freshly baked.
- Baguettes develop more flavour if you chill the dough overnight in the refrigerator. After the dough has risen in step 2, gently fold dough over itself to deflate it, cover the bowl with cling film and store it in the refrigerator. The next day proceed with step 3 as directed by the recipe. The baguettes may need 10-20 minutes longer to rise in step 4 before baking.

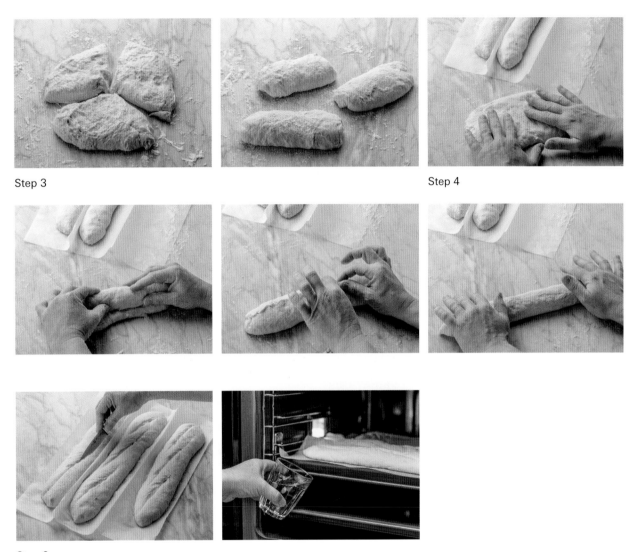

Step 3

Step 4

Step 6

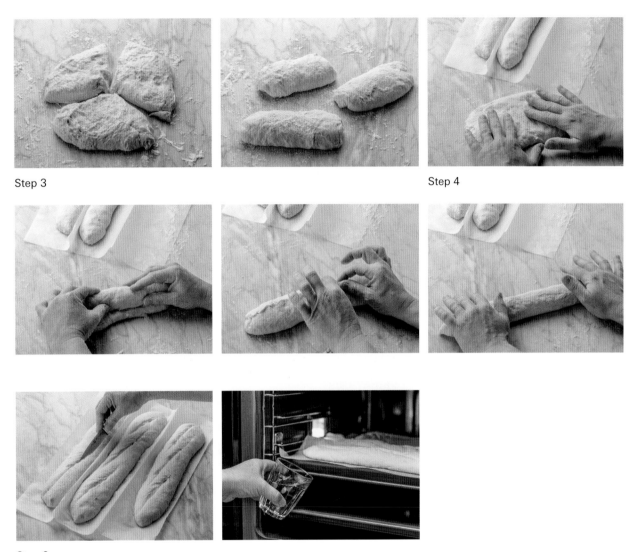

MILK BREAD

INGREDIENTS

50 g butter, cut into pieces,
    plus extra for greasing
300 g milk
20 g fresh yeast, crumbled or
    2 tsp dried instant yeast (8 g)
20-60 g sugar
550 g bread flour
1½ tsp salt
1 egg, lightly whisked, for glazing

USEFUL ITEMS

cling film or kitchen towel
baking tray and paper
pastry brush

PREPARATION

1. Lightly grease a large bowl and set aside. Place milk, butter, fresh yeast and sugar into mixing bowl and warm **3 min/37°C/speed 2**.
2. Add bread flour and salt and knead **3 min/🌾**. Place dough into prepared bowl, cover with cling film or a damp kitchen towel and let rise in a warm place until doubled in size (approx. 1 hour).
3. Line a baking tray with baking paper and set aside. Divide dough into 3 pieces and roll each piece into a rope (approx. 45 cm). Join the 3 ropes at one end, plait, and join again at the other end. Place plait onto prepared baking tray, cover with cling film or a damp kitchen towel and let rise again in a warm place until doubled in size (approx. 30 minutes). Meanwhile, preheat oven to 180°C.
4. Brush with whisked egg and bake for 25-30 minutes (180°C) or until bread sounds hollow when tapped on the underside. Allow to cool on a cooling rack before slicing.

TIP

- The dough will be slightly sticky. If the dough seems very wet after step 2, add a tablespoon of flour and knead a further **30 sec/🌾**.

VARIATIONS

- Sprinkle with flaked almonds or pearl sugar after brushing with egg.
- One minute before the end of step 2, add 80 g raisins.
- Form dough into small men, using raisins for eyes and buttons.

 20 min   2 h 20 min   medium   30 / 30 slices   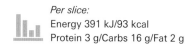 Per slice:
Energy 391 kJ/93 kcal
Protein 3 g/Carbs 16 g/Fat 2 g

Step 3

BRIOCHE

INGREDIENTS

20 g milk

20 g fresh yeast, crumbled or
2 tsp dried instant yeast (8 g)

350 g bread flour,
plus extra for dusting

4 eggs

60-100 g sugar

1 tsp salt

170 g butter, unsalted, cut into
pieces, plus extra for greasing

1 egg yolk, lightly whisked,
for glazing

USEFUL ITEMS

cling film or kitchen towel
loaf tin (approx. 28 cm long)
pastry brush
cooling rack

PREPARATION

1. Place milk and fresh yeast into mixing bowl and warm
   1 min/37°C/speed 2.
2. Add bread flour, 4 eggs, sugar and salt and knead **10 min/**⚘ while
   adding butter little by little through hole in mixing bowl lid onto
   rotating blades.
3. Transfer dough into a large bowl, cover with cling film or a damp
   kitchen towel and let rise in a warm place until doubled in size
   (approx. 3 hours).
4. Grease a loaf tin (approx. 28 cm long) and set aside. Transfer dough
   onto a lightly floured surface and gently flatten with floured hands to
   form a rough rectangle. Roll the rectangle of dough into a log shape
   the length of the loaf tin. Place dough into prepared loaf tin, seam side
   down, and cover with cling film or a damp kitchen towel. Let loaf rise
   in a warm place until doubled in size (approx. 1 hour). Meanwhile,
   preheat oven to 180°C.
5. Brush surface with egg yolk and bake for 30 minutes (180°C) or until
   dark golden brown. Remove brioche from loaf tin and allow to cool on
   a cooling rack before slicing.

TIP

• You can refrigerate the dough for easier shaping. After step 3, gently fold dough
over itself to deflate it, cover bowl with cling film and place in refrigerator. Continue
with the recipe at your convenience up to 24 hours later, allowing more time for
the loaf to rise in step 4.

Variation: Brioche à tête

 20 min   5 h   medium   16
                                                                     16 slices

Per slice:
Energy 669 kJ/160 kcal
Protein 4 g/Carbs 16 g/Fat 9 g

VARIATION

- **Brioche à tête** (traditional French brioche shape): divide dough into 2 pieces, one large ($^4/_5$ of the final loaf) and one small ($^1/_5$). Form both pieces into smooth balls. Place the large ball into a greased fluted brioche tin, and using your fingers, create a deep indentation in the middle until your fingers are touching the bottom of the tin. Roll the small ball of dough into a tear-drop shape, with a longer, pointy part. Place the pointy part of the small piece of dough into the indentation of the large ball, forming a "head", and push down deeply all around the head to tuck it firmly into the large ball of dough. Let rise, then bake as directed by the recipe.

SAUCES, DIPS AND SPREADS – SAVOURY

TOMATO SAUCE

INGREDIENTS

120 g onions, cut into halves
1 garlic clove
50 g extra virgin olive oil
800 g crushed tomatoes, canned
1 tsp sugar
½ tsp salt (adjust to taste)
5-10 fresh basil leaves

PREPARATION

1. Place onions, garlic clove and extra virgin olive oil into mixing bowl. Chop **5 sec/speed 5**, then sauté **7 min/120°C/speed 1**.
2. Add tomatoes, sugar, salt and basil. Cook **20 min/100°C/speed 2**. Serve hot with pasta or as a sauce for vegetables.

VARIATION

- **Fresh tomato sauce:** instead of crushed tomatoes, use 800 g fresh plum tomatoes, cut into pieces. After adding the ingredients in step 2, chop **15 sec/speed 5** and proceed with recipe, extending cooking time to 30 minutes, and placing simmering basket instead of measuring cup onto mixing bowl lid to help prevent splashing.

 10 min   40 min  easy 1 total recipe (approx. 450 g)  Per recipe: Energy 2723 kJ/648 kcal Protein 12 g/Carbs 33 g/Fat 52 g

VEGETABLE PASTA SAUCE

INGREDIENTS

100 g onions, cut into halves

1 garlic clove

20 g olive oil

60 g carrots, cut into pieces

300 g courgettes, cut into pieces

100 g button mushrooms,
    cut into pieces

500 g chopped tomatoes,
    canned or fresh

½ tsp salt

¼ tsp ground black pepper,
    adjust to taste

1 tsp dried basil

1 tsp butter

8 fresh basil leaves, torn into pieces

1-2 tbsp fresh parsley, leaves only,
    chopped (optional)

Grated Parmesan cheese (optional)

PREPARATION

1. Place onions and garlic clove into mixing bowl and chop **3 sec/speed 5**. Scrape down sides of mixing bowl with spatula.
2. Add olive oil and sauté **3 min/120°C/speed 1**.
3. Add carrots and chop **5 sec/speed 5**.
4. Add courgettes and button mushrooms and chop **4 sec/speed 4**.
5. Add chopped tomatoes, salt, black pepper, dried basil, butter, fresh basil and fresh parsley and cook **25 min/100°C/↻/speed 2**. Season with salt to taste and serve hot, with grated Parmesan cheese.

TIP
• Serve with any type of pasta.

 10 min 40 min easy 4 portions 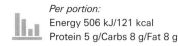 *Per portion:* Energy 506 kJ/121 kcal Protein 5 g/Carbs 8 g/Fat 8 g

BASIL PESTO

INGREDIENTS

80 g Parmesan cheese,
    cut into pieces
30 g pine nuts
1 garlic clove (optional)
80 g fresh basil leaves
150 g extra virgin olive oil
½ tsp salt

USEFUL ITEMS

1 jam jar with twist-off lid

PREPARATION

1. Place Parmesan cheese into mixing bowl and grate **15 sec/speed 10**.
2. Add pine nuts, garlic clove, basil leaves, extra virgin olive oil and salt and chop **20 sec/speed 7**. Serve as a sauce or transfer into a jar with a twist-off lid and store in refrigerator.

TIPS
- Serve with spaghetti or other types of pasta. If you prefer a thinner sauce, add 1-2 tbsp cooking water from the pasta and mix before serving.
- To keep pesto fresh in the refrigerator for up to a month, place into a clean jar, cover with a layer of olive oil and seal the jar air-tight.

VARIATION
- For a greater depth of flavour, replace 30 g of the Parmesan cheese with 30 g pecorino cheese.

 10 min   10 min   easy    1 total recipe (approx. 350 g)    *Per recipe:* Energy 7741 kJ/1848 kcal Protein 34 g/Carbs 7 g/Fat 190 g

BÉCHAMEL SAUCE

INGREDIENTS

40 g butter
40 g flour
500 g milk
½ tsp salt
2 pinches ground black pepper
2 pinches ground nutmeg (optional)

PREPARATION

1. Place butter into mixing bowl and melt **3 min/100°C/speed 1**.
2. Add flour and cook **3 min/100°C/speed 1**.
3. Add milk, salt, black pepper and nutmeg and cook **6 min/90°C/speed 4**. Serve béchamel sauce immediately or use as needed.

TIPS

• Quick version: Place all ingredients into mixing bowl and cook **7 min/90°C/speed 4**. The main version has a little more flavour, but this faster version is an acceptable substitute.
• Béchamel sauce can be used in many dishes such as gratins, lasagne, or vol-au-vents (puff pastry shells with savoury filling).

VARIATION

• Béchamel sauce is the base for several other sauces. For example:
  – **Mornay sauce:** add 50 g grated cheese at the end of step 3 (you may also add 2 egg yolks and 20 g cream), then mix **15 sec/speed 4**.
  – **Aurore sauce:** add 1 tsp tomato paste to the béchamel at the end of step 3 and mix **15 sec/speed 4**.

Tip

 5 min   15 min   easy    1 total recipe (approx. 580 g)    *Per recipe:* Energy 3203 kJ/766 kcal Protein 21 g/Carbs 53 g/Fat 52 g

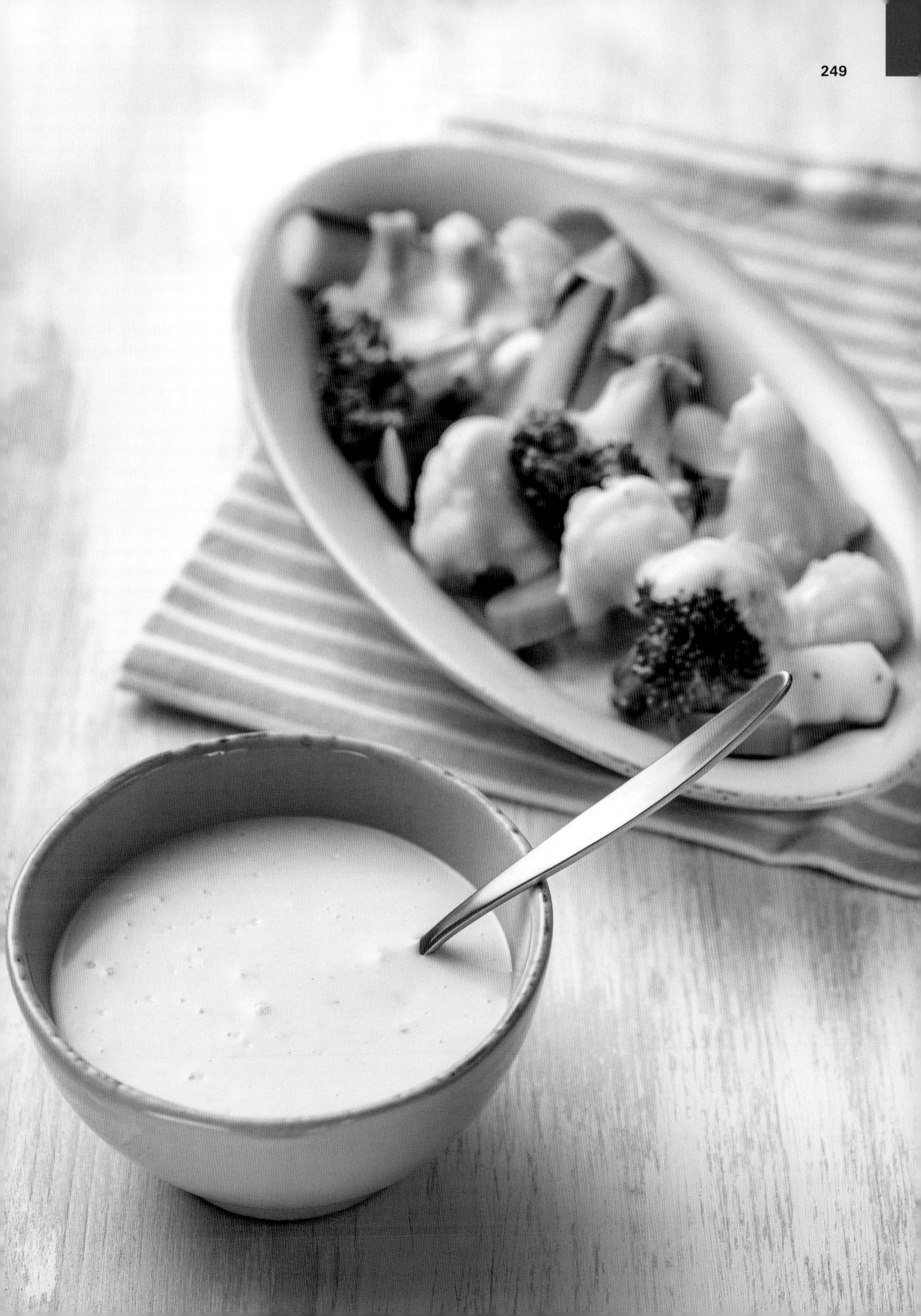

HOLLANDAISE SAUCE

INGREDIENTS

250 g butter, unsalted, cut into
    pieces
50 g water
1 tbsp lemon juice
3 egg yolks
½ tsp salt
1 pinch freshly ground pepper

PREPARATION

1. Place butter into mixing bowl and melt **4 min/70°C/speed 2**. Transfer into a jug and set aside.
2. **Insert butterfly whisk.** Place water, lemon juice, egg yolks, salt and pepper into mixing bowl and heat **2 min/70°C/speed 4**.
3. Mix **4-5 min/70°C/speed 4** while very slowly pouring melted butter onto mixing bowl lid, letting it drizzle around measuring cup in a thin stream onto rotating blades to create an emulsion. Serve immediately.

TIPS

- If the sauce seems too thin, emulsify for slightly longer in step 3.
- If the sauce becomes too thick, add 2 tbsp water and mix **30 sec/70°C/speed 2** before serving.
- Hollandaise sauce goes well with steamed asparagus, small potatoes, vegetables or fish. Steam the dish first, then prepare the hollandaise sauce and serve warm.
- Hollandaise sauce is best served freshly made. Leftovers can be gently warmed in the Thermomix™ at 70°C before serving.

VARIATION

- **Maltese sauce:** replace lemon juice with orange juice.

 10 min   15 min   easy    1 total recipe (approx. 350 g)    *Per recipe:* Energy 8751 kJ/2093 kcal Protein 11 g/Carbs 1 g/Fat 227 g

BÉARNAISE SAUCE

INGREDIENTS

50 g shallots, cut into halves

1 sprig fresh tarragon, leaves only

50 g dry white wine

1 tbsp white wine vinegar
(preferably tarragon vinegar)

200 g butter, unsalted, cut into
pieces

4 egg yolks

1 tsp salt

1 pinch ground black pepper

PREPARATION

1. Place shallots and tarragon into mixing bowl and chop **5 sec/speed 5**. Scrape down sides of mixing bowl with spatula.
2. Add white wine and vinegar and cook **5 min/90°C/speed 2**.
3. Add butter, egg yolks, salt and black pepper and emulsify **4 min/70°C/speed 4**. Transfer into a bowl and serve hot.

TIP
• Serve with red meat, grilled or roasted.

 10 min   15 min   easy  1 total recipe (approx. 380 g)  *Per 1 total recipe:* Energy 7666 kJ/1833 kcal Protein 15 g/Carbs 2 g/Fat 192 g

MAYONNAISE

INGREDIENTS

250 g sunflower oil
1 egg
1 tsp lemon juice or vinegar
2 tsp mustard (10 g) (optional)
2 pinches ground black pepper
    (optional)
½ tsp salt

USEFUL ITEMS

jug
air-tight jar

PREPARATION

1. Place a jug onto mixing bowl lid, weigh sunflower oil into jug and set aside.
2. Place egg, lemon juice, mustard, pepper and salt into mixing bowl. Mix **1 min 30 sec/speed 4** while very slowly pouring reserved sunflower oil onto mixing bowl lid, letting it drizzle around measuring cup in a thin stream onto rotating blades to create an emulsion. Transfer mayonnaise into a bowl and serve immediately or transfer into an air-tight jar and store in refrigerator.

TIPS

- For best results, all ingredients and mixing bowl should be at room temperature.
- If mayonnaise does not thicken, transfer into a bowl and set aside. Place an additional egg into mixing bowl and mix **1 min 30 sec/speed 4** while very slowly pouring reserved mayonnaise mixture onto mixing bowl lid, letting it drizzle in a thin stream onto rotating blades.

VARIATION

- **Garlic mayonnaise:** start by placing 1-2 garlic cloves into the empty mixing bowl, chop **3 sec/speed 8** and leave chopped garlic in mixing bowl. Proceed as directed by the recipe.

Tip

 5 min   5 min   easy    1 total recipe (approx. 300 g)   *Per recipe:* Energy 9570 kJ/2287 kcal Protein 7 g/Carbs 1 g/Fat 255 g

EGG FREE MAYONNAISE

INGREDIENTS

300 g sunflower oil or olive oil
150 g milk
1 garlic clove (optional)
½ tsp salt, adjust to taste
1 tbsp lemon juice or 1 tsp vinegar
(optional)

USEFUL ITEMS

jug
air-tight jar

PREPARATION

1. Place a jug onto mixing bowl lid, weigh sunflower oil into jug and set aside.
2. Place milk, garlic clove and salt into mixing bowl and chop **1 min/37°C/speed 5**.
3. Mix **3 min/37°C/speed 5** while very slowly pouring reserved oil onto mixing bowl lid, letting it drizzle around measuring cup in a thin stream onto rotating blades to create an emulsion.
4. Add lemon juice and mix **5 sec/speed 5**. Transfer into a bowl and serve immediately or transfer into an air-tight jar and store in refrigerator.

TIPS

- For a more fluid mayonnaise, add 50-100 g milk after step 4 and mix **3 sec/speed 5**.
- You can add some mustard to give the mayonnaise extra flavour and colour.

 10 min 10 min 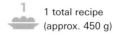 easy 1 total recipe (approx. 450 g)  *Per 1 total recipe:* Energy 11508 kJ/2750 kcal Protein 5 g/Carbs 7 g/Fat 305 g

TOMATO KETCHUP

INGREDIENTS

1000 g ripe tomatoes, cut into
    quarters, or canned whole
    tomatoes
180 g red peppers, cut into pieces
130 g red onions
2 garlic cloves
100 g red wine vinegar
1 bay leaf, fresh
1 pinch ground nutmeg
¼ tsp ground black pepper
¼-½ tsp chilli powder
1 tsp paprika
1 tsp salt
100 g honey

USEFUL ITEMS

bottles or jam jars with twist-off lids

PREPARATION

1. Place tomatoes, red peppers, onions, garlic cloves and 50 g vinegar into mixing bowl and chop **5 sec/speed 7**.
2. Add bay leaf and cook **40 min/100°C/speed 2**, placing simmering basket instead of measuring cup onto mixing bowl lid to help prevent splashing.
3. Remove bay leaf and add remaining 50 g vinegar, nutmeg, black pepper, chilli powder, paprika, salt and honey. Insert measuring cup and cook **15 min/Varoma/speed 1**. Adjust seasoning to taste.
4. Blend **1 min/speed 3-7, increasing speed gradually**. Transfer into sterilised bottles or jam jars and close air-tight. Allow to cool, then serve or store in refrigerator.

TIPS
- Provided the bottles have been thoroughly washed and rinsed with boiling water, this sauce can be stored in the refrigerator for up to 3 months.
- If sauce seems too liquid after cooking in step 3, reduce a further **10 min/Varoma/speed 1** or longer, until desired consistency is achieved.
- The flavour improves with time. If possible, keep it refrigerated for two weeks before serving.

 15 min   1 h 15 min   easy    1 total recipe (approx. 1200 g)   *Per portion:* Energy 218 kJ/52 kcal Protein 1 g/Carbs 10 g/Fat 0 g

CURRY KETCHUP

INGREDIENTS

150 g pickled gherkins,
    cut into pieces
150 g onions, cut into halves
60 g butter
40 g sugar
4 heaped tbsp curry powder (40 g)
    (e.g. Zanzibar or Madras curry
    powder)
1000 g crushed tomatoes, canned
500 g tomato ketchup
70 g tomato purée (concentrated)
2 tsp salt, plus extra to taste
2 tsp sambal oelek (20 g)
1 heaped tsp meat stock paste,
    homemade, or 1 meat stock
    cube (for 0.5 l)
20 g fruit vinegar

USEFUL ITEMS

4 jam jars with twist-off lids

PREPARATION

1. Place pickled gherkins into mixing bowl and chop **2-3 sec/speed 5**. Transfer into a bowl and set aside.
2. Place onions into mixing bowl and chop **5 sec/speed 5**. Scrape down sides of mixing bowl with spatula.
3. Add butter and sugar and sauté **3 min/120°C/speed 1**.
4. Add curry powder and sauté **2 min/120°C/speed 2**.
5. Add crushed tomatoes, tomato ketchup, tomato purée, salt, sambal oelek, meat stock paste, fruit vinegar and reserved chopped gherkins and cook **15 min/100°C/✿/speed 3.5**. Adjust seasoning to taste. Transfer hot sauce into four sterilised jam jars with twist-off lids and close immediately air-tight. Allow to cool, then serve or store in refrigerator.

TIPS

• Serve over grilled sausages (e.g. Bratwurst), or with grilled meats or meat fondue.
• For a milder sauce, use only 1 tsp sambal oelek.
• Makes 4 x 450 g jars. Refrigerated sauce stays fresh for a few weeks.
• One jar is enough for approx. 6 sausages.

 15 min   30 min   medium  4 jars (450 g each)  *Per 1 jar:* Energy 1680 kJ/401 kcal Protein 8 g/Carbs 56 g/Fat 15 g

MUSTARD-DILL SAUCE

INGREDIENTS

200 g rapeseed oil

10-15 g fresh dill, leaves only

20-30 g sugar (caster sugar),
   to taste

20 g white wine vinegar

20 g lemon juice

25 g Dijon mustard or other
   medium hot mustard

30 g sweet mustard

1 egg yolk

½ tsp salt

¼ tsp ground black pepper

USEFUL ITEMS

jug

PREPARATION

1. Place a jug onto mixing bowl lid, weigh rapeseed oil into jug and set aside.

2. Place dill into mixing bowl and chop **5 sec/speed 8**. Transfer into a bowl and set aside.

3. Place sugar, white wine vinegar, lemon juice, Dijon mustard, sweet mustard, egg yolk, salt and black pepper into mixing bowl and mix **5 sec/speed 4**.

4. Mix on **speed 3** while very slowly pouring oil onto mixing bowl lid, letting it drizzle around measuring cup in a thin stream onto rotating blades to create an emulsion.

5. Add reserved chopped dill, mix **8 sec/⟲/speed 3** and refrigerate for at least 2 hours. Serve cold.

TIP
• Serve this sauce with salmon (e.g. gravlax) or boiled eggs.

VARIATION
• Instead of rapeseed oil use another neutral oil (e.g. safflower oil, sunflower oil).

  10 min   2 h 15 min   easy    1 total recipe (approx. 350 g)    *Per portion:* Energy 1068 kJ/255 kcal Protein 1 g/Carbs 4 g/Fat 26 g

MUSTARD BALSAMIC VINEGAR DRESSING

INGREDIENTS

240 g extra virgin olive oil

50 g wholegrain mustard

50 g balsamic vinegar

2 tsp sugar (caster sugar) (optional)

2 tbsp mixed dried herbs (e.g. basil, oregano, thyme, rosemary)

1 tsp salt

¼ tsp freshly ground black pepper

USEFUL ITEMS

jug

air-tight jar

PREPARATION

1. Place a jug onto mixing bowl lid, weigh extra virgin olive oil into jug and set aside.
2. Place wholegrain mustard, balsamic vinegar, sugar, mixed dried herbs, salt and black pepper into mixing bowl and mix **30 sec/speed 4**.
3. Mix **3 min/speed 4** while very slowly pouring extra virgin olive oil onto mixing bowl lid, letting it drizzle around measuring cup in a thin stream onto rotating blades to create an emulsion. Serve or transfer into an air-tight jar and store in refrigerator.

TIPS

- Use dressing on green leaf salads or salads combining chopped raw vegetables and fruit.
- This dressing keeps for several weeks in the refrigerator.

VARIATION

- Create your own dressing, using this recipe as a basic guideline. Try different types of oil and vinegar and add seasonings and flavours of your choice.

 10 min 10 min easy  1 total recipe (approx. 350 g)  *Per recipe:* Energy 9420 kJ/2249 kcal Protein 4 g/Carbs 15 g/Fat 245 g

ORANGE CURRY DRESSING

INGREDIENTS

200 g walnut oil or other nut oil

1-2 oranges, preferably organic, zest and juice

30 g shallots

20 g hot mustard

½ tsp curry powder

½ tsp salt

20 g fruit vinegar (e. g. apple, peach)

USEFUL ITEMS

jug

air-tight jar

PREPARATION

1. Place a jug onto mixing bowl lid, weigh walnut oil into jug and set aside.
2. Place 130 g freshly squeezed orange juice, a strip of orange zest (1 x 3 cm), shallots, hot mustard, curry powder, salt and fruit vinegar into mixing bowl and chop **20 sec/speed 8**.
3. Mix **3 min/speed 4** while very slowly pouring walnut oil onto mixing bowl lid, letting it drizzle around measuring cup in a thin stream onto rotating blades to create an emulsion. Serve or transfer into an air-tight jar and store in refrigerator.

TIPS

- Use dressing on green leaf salads or salads combining chopped raw vegetables and fruit.
- This dressing keeps for up to a week in the refrigerator.

VARIATION

- Create your own dressing, using this recipe as a basic guideline. Try different types of oil and vinegar and add seasonings and flavours of your choice.

 10 min 10 min easy  1 jar (approx. 380 g)  *Per jar:* Energy 7791 kJ/1862 kcal Protein 23 g/Carbs 15 g/Fat 201 g

YOGHURT DRESSING

INGREDIENTS

200 g plain yoghurt
2 tsp mustard, preferably sweet
    (10 g)
50 g sunflower oil
1½ tbsp lemon juice (25 g)
1½ tsp honey (10 g)
50 g apple juice or other fruit juice
1 pinch salt
1 pinch freshly ground black pepper

USEFUL ITEMS

air-tight jar

PREPARATION

1. Place plain yoghurt, mustard, sunflower oil, lemon juice, honey, apple juice, salt and black pepper into mixing bowl and mix **10 sec/speed 5**. Serve or transfer into an air-tight jar and store in refrigerator.

TIPS

• Use dressing on green leaf salads or salads combining chopped raw vegetables and fruit.
• This dressing keeps for up to 3 days in the refrigerator.

VARIATION

• Create your own dressing, using this recipe as a basic guideline. Try different types of oil and fruit juice and add seasonings and flavours of your choice.

 5 min 5 min easy  1 total recipe (approx. 350 g)  *Per jar:* Energy 2726 kJ/651 kcal Protein 9 g/Carbs 23 g/Fat 58 g

MANGO CHUTNEY

INGREDIENTS

1 tbsp Sichuan peppercorns
    or 2 tsp black peppercorns
    + 1 tsp finely grated lemon zest
2 garlic cloves
10 g fresh ginger, cut into thin
    slices
80 g onions, cut into halves
20 g water
250 g raw cane sugar
700 g mangoes, flesh only,
    cut into pieces
120 g vinegar
1 tsp salt
½ tsp ground turmeric
100 g raisins

USEFUL ITEMS

2 jam jars with twist-off lids

PREPARATION

1. Place Sichuan peppercorns into mixing bowl and toast
   6 min/Varoma/↺/speed 1, then grind **25 sec/speed 10**.
   Transfer into a bowl and set aside.
2. Place garlic cloves and ginger into mixing bowl and chop
   2 sec/speed 8. Scrape down sides of mixing bowl with spatula.
3. Add onions and chop **3 sec/speed 5**. Transfer into a bowl and
   set aside.
4. Place water and raw cane sugar into mixing bowl and cook
   5 min/100°C/speed 1.
5. Add reserved ground Sichuan pepper, reserved ginger-onion mixture,
   mangoes, vinegar, salt, turmeric and raisins and cook
   45 min/100°C/speed 1, placing simmering basket instead of
   measuring cup onto mixing bowl lid to help prevent splashing.
6. Remove simmering basket, insert measuring cup and mix
   10 sec/speed 4. Pour into 2 sterilised jam jars with twist-off lids
   and close immediately. Turn jam jars upside down for 10 minutes
   before turning right side up. Allow to cool and serve or store in a cool,
   dry place.

TIPS
- Serve with cheese or as a condiment for meat or fish or with an Indian curry meal.
- After opening, store jar in the refrigerator.

VARIATION
- Replace mangoes with apples, pears, plums, apricots or papayas.

 10 min   1 h 20 min    easy    1 total recipe (approx. 1000 g)

Per jar:
Energy 3736 kJ/886 kcal
Protein 5 g/Carbs 205 g/Fat 2 g

GUACAMOLE

INGREDIENTS

90 g onions, cut into halves

1 serrano chilli or fresh chilli, deseeded

20 g lime juice or lemon juice

½-1 tsp salt, to taste

10 g olive oil

2-3 sprigs fresh coriander, leaves only

200 g tomatoes, cut into quarters

500 g avocado (2-3 avocados), ripe, cut into pieces

PREPARATION

1. Place onions, serrano chilli, lime juice, salt, olive oil and coriander into the mixing bowl and chop **5 sec/speed 5**.
2. Add tomatoes and chop **3 sec/speed 5**.
3. Add avocado and mix **5-10 sec/⟳/speed 5**. Adjust seasoning to taste. Serve immediately or refrigerate until ready to serve.

TIPS

- Serve with tortilla chips or crackers.
- Replace fresh chilli with ¼-1 tsp dried chilli powder or cayenne pepper, to taste.
- Adjust mixing time in step 3 according to the ripeness of the avocado and desired guacamole texture.
- To prevent browning, garnish the guacamole with an avocado stone, tomato slices, or cover with cling film in direct contact with the guacamole.

 5 min   5 min    easy   1 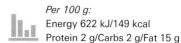 1 total recipe (approx. 830 g)   *Per 100 g:* Energy 622 kJ/149 kcal Protein 2 g/Carbs 2 g/Fat 15 g

TZATZIKI

INGREDIENTS

350 g cucumbers, peeled,
   deseeded, cut into pieces

1 tsp salt, plus extra to taste

2 garlic cloves

5 sprigs fresh dill

20 g olive oil

350 g Greek yoghurt, 10% fat,
   or plain yoghurt

15 g lemon juice or vinegar
   (optional)

½ tsp ground black pepper

PREPARATION

1. Place cucumber and salt into mixing bowl and chop **3 sec/speed 5**. Transfer cucumber into simmering basket and drain for approx. 10 minutes. Using a large spoon or your hands, squeeze as much water out of the chopped cucumber as possible. Set aside.

2. Place garlic cloves, dill and olive oil into mixing bowl and chop **3 sec/speed 5**.

3. Add reserved chopped cucumbers, Greek yoghurt, lemon juice and black pepper and mix **20 sec/❤/speed 2.5**. Adjust seasoning, transfer tzatziki into a bowl and refrigerate before serving.

TIP
• Serve tzatziki with pitta bread, crusty bread, grilled meat or baked potatoes.

VARIATIONS
• The cucumbers may be left unpeeled.
• Replace Greek yoghurt with a combination of 200 g plain yoghurt (3.5% fat) and 200 g curd cheese (20% fat).

 10 min   20 min   easy 4 / 4 portions

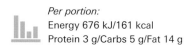
Per portion:
Energy 676 kJ/161 kcal
Protein 3 g/Carbs 5 g/Fat 14 g

CREAM CHEESE SPREAD WITH RADISHES

INGREDIENTS

3-4 tbsp garden cress (10 g),
   roots removed, or fresh
   chives (10 g), chopped
60-80 g red radishes
200 g cream cheese
¼ tsp salt
¼ tsp ground black pepper

PREPARATION

1. Place garden cress into mixing bowl, reserving 1 tbsp for garnish. Add red radishes and chop **3 sec/speed 5**.
2. Add cream cheese, salt and black pepper and mix **10 sec/speed 3**. Garnish with reserved garden cress and serve.

VARIATIONS
• Replace red radishes with any variety of radish.
• Garden cress can also be replaced with 3-4 tbsp watercress.

 5 min   5 min   easy   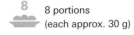 8 portions (each approx. 30 g)   *Per portion:* Energy 361 kJ/86 kcal Protein 3 g/Carbs 1 g/Fat 8 g

SAUCES, DIPS AND SPREADS – SWEET

APPLE SAUCE

INGREDIENTS

750 g apples, cut into pieces
20 g lemon juice, adjust to taste
50 g sugar, adjust to taste
1 tsp vanilla sugar,
    homemade (optional)

PREPARATION

1. Place apples, lemon juice, sugar and vanilla sugar into mixing bowl and cook **9 min/100°C/speed 1**.
2. Purée **20 sec/speed 5** or until desired consistency is achieved. Transfer into a bowl and serve hot or cold.

TIPS

- This sauce goes well with rice pudding, pancakes, potato cakes or with roasted or grilled pork.
- If you use unpeeled apples, purée a few seconds longer.
- If you like apple sauce with a chunkier texture, purée for a shorter amount of time or do not purée at all and serve as stewed apples.

VARIATIONS

- Sprinkle with a mixture of sugar and cinnamon.
- Instead of apples use other kinds of fruit or a mixture of fruits.

 10 min   20 min   easy   6 portions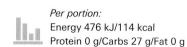

Per portion:
Energy 476 kJ/114 kcal
Protein 0 g/Carbs 27 g/Fat 0 g

FRUIT SAUCE (COULIS)

INGREDIENTS

250 g fresh fruit
    (e. g. berries, mango),
    room temperature,
    cut into pieces as needed

75 g sugar (caster sugar),
    adjust to taste

15 g lemon juice

PREPARATION

1. Place fresh fruit, sugar and lemon juice into mixing bowl and blend **30 sec/speed 5-10, increasing speed gradually**. Scrape down sides of mixing bowl with spatula.

2. Cook **5 min/90°C/speed 2**. Allow sauce to cool before serving.

TIPS

- Serve this sauce with ice cream, hot or cold desserts, Bavarian cream, cakes, roast meats, etc.
- For a smoother consistency, strain the sauce through a fine-meshed strainer.
- If the fruit is very ripe or sweet, the sugar can be adjusted or omitted completely.
- If using less juicy fruit, such as bananas, mangoes or papayas, add 50-75 g water to achieve consistency as desired.
- The coulis keeps well in a sealed glass container in the refrigerator for up to a week.

 10 min   10 min   easy    1 total recipe (320 g)   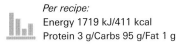 *Per recipe:* Energy 1719 kJ/411 kcal Protein 3 g/Carbs 95 g/Fat 1 g

VANILLA SAUCE (CRÈME ANGLAISE)

INGREDIENTS

300 g milk
4 egg yolks
1 pinch salt (optional)
50 g sugar
½ vanilla pod

PREPARATION

1. **Insert butterfly whisk.** Place milk, egg yolks, salt and sugar into mixing bowl. Split vanilla pod lengthwise and scrape out seeds. Add seeds and vanilla pod into mixing bowl and heat **7 min/80°C/↻/speed 2**. Pour sauce into a bowl, remove vanilla pod and serve sauce warm or cold.

TIPS

- This is a very liquid custard, which thickens a little as it cools. If the mixture seems too liquid, heat for a further **2 min/80°C/↻/speed 2**.
- Replace the vanilla pod and 50 g sugar with 50 g homemade vanilla sugar.
- Serve sauce with chocolate ice cream, fruit crumble, apple strudel or yeast dumplings.
- Serve sauce cold with a red berry sauce over fresh fruit.

Step 1

 5 min 10 min easy 4 portions  *Per portion:* Energy 706 kJ/169 kcal Protein 6 g/Carbs 16 g/Fat 9 g

CHOCOLATE SAUCE (SYRUP)

INGREDIENTS

250 g sugar
½ vanilla pod, cut into pieces
250 g water
1 pinch salt
100 g cocoa powder

PREPARATION

1. Place sugar and vanilla pod into mixing bowl and grind **25 sec/speed 10**.
2. Add water and salt into mixing bowl and reduce **9 min/Varoma/speed 2**, placing simmering basket instead of measuring cup onto mixing bowl lid to help prevent splashing.
3. Add cocoa powder and reduce for a further **4 min/Varoma/speed 4**, placing simmering basket instead of measuring cup onto mixing bowl lid. Transfer chocolate sauce into a bottle or small carafe and serve hot or cold.

TIPS

- Serve with desserts such as ice cream, semolina pudding, vanilla pudding, fresh fruit, pancakes, etc.
- Many allergy sufferers can tolerate this sauce, as it is dairy-free and nut-free.
- This chocolate sauce will keep for weeks in the refrigerator.
- Add 200 g milk to any sauce remaining in the mixing bowl and heat **3 min/80°C/speed 2** to enjoy a delicious hot chocolate drink.

VARIATION

- To make a thicker chocolate spread for bread, after step 3 reduce chocolate sauce for a further **2-3 min/Varoma/speed 2**, placing simmering basket instead of measuring cup onto mixing bowl lid.

 5 min   20 min   easy    1 total recipe (approx. 500 g)   *Per recipe:* Energy 5597 kJ/1338 kcal Protein 23 g/Carbs 268 g/Fat 20 g

CHOCOLATE HAZELNUT SPREAD

INGREDIENTS

60 g hazelnuts

60 g sugar

1 tsp vanilla sugar, homemade

10-20 g cocoa powder

90 g milk

170 g milk chocolate, cut into
   pieces

60 g peanut oil or sunflower oil
   (optional)

USEFUL ITEMS

baking tray

air-tight jar (approx. 450 g)

PREPARATION

1. Preheat oven to 160°C. Roast hazelnuts on a baking tray for 10 minutes and allow to cool a little.
2. Place sugar and vanilla sugar into mixing bowl and grind **20 sec/speed 10**.
3. Add reserved roasted hazelnuts and cocoa powder grind **20 sec/speed 10**. Scrape down sides of mixing bowl with spatula.
4. Add milk and heat **4 min/100°C/speed 4**, then blend **2 min/speed 10**. Scrape down sides of mixing bowl with spatula.
5. Add milk chocolate and peanut oil and melt **3 min/50°C/speed 3**.
6. Transfer into a sterilised jar and close air-tight. Allow to cool, then serve or refrigerate until needed.

TIPS
• Replace vanilla sugar with ½ tsp natural vanilla extract, adding it in step 5.
• Store the hazelnut spread in the refrigerator for a few weeks, or for a few days at room temperature.

VARIATION
• Replace part of the milk chocolate with dark chocolate, as desired.
• The peanut oil can be omitted for a more intensely flavoured spread, however the texture will not be as velvety smooth.

 10 min   45 min    easy   1   1 jar (approx. 450 g)    *Per jar:* Energy 9214 kJ/2201 kcal Protein 32 g/Carbs 167 g/Fat 158 g

TRADITIONAL FRUIT JAM

INGREDIENTS

500 g fruit, cut into pieces as
needed
30 g lemon juice
500 g sugar

USEFUL ITEMS

jam jars with twist-off lids

PREPARATION

1. Place fruit, lemon juice and sugar into mixing bowl and blend **10 sec/speed 6**. Cook **28 min/Varoma/speed 1** (90°C for strawberry jam, see variation), placing simmering basket instead of measuring cup onto mixing bowl lid to help prevent splashing.

2. Test setting point of jam (see tip), pour into sterilised jam jars with twist-off lids and seal immediately. Turn jam jars upside down for 10 minutes before turning right side up and allowing to cool. Serve or store in a cool dry place.

TIPS

- Only use ripe fruit in this recipe.
- Setting point test: place a saucer into the freezer (5-10 minutes). Place 1 tsp jam onto the chilled saucer. When jam on saucer is cool, push it with your finger. If the jam wrinkles, it is ready. If not, boil jam for a further 2 minutes, then test again.
- To ensure preservation, clean jam jars thoroughly in hot soapy water, then dry in a low oven or run them through the dishwasher. Pour jam into jars while jars are still warm and proceed as directed by the recipe.
- This is a traditional jam recipe with sugar acting as the only conservation and thickening agent. Thanks to the high sugar content, this jam can be stored on a shelf for several months. Once opened, this jam will keep in the refrigerator for up to 1 month.

VARIATIONS

- You can use any fruit or fruit combination for this recipe.
- With certain fruit such as strawberries, the jam may bubble up onto the mixing bowl lid. If this happens, reduce temperature to 100°C or even to 90°C as needed.
- **Strawberry jam:** include 1 apple (150 g) in the 500 g fruit. The pectin in the apple will help the jam reach setting point faster.

  15 min 55 min  easy 1 total recipe (approx. 800 g) 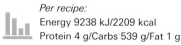 *Per recipe:* Energy 9238 kJ/2209 kcal Protein 4 g/Carbs 539 g/Fat 1 g

Tip

LEMON CURD

INGREDIENTS

240 g sugar

3-5 lemons, zest and juice,
    preferably organic

120 g butter, unsalted,
    cut into pieces

3 eggs

USEFUL ITEMS

2 jam jars with twist-off lids

PREPARATION

1. Place sugar and zest of 1 lemon into mixing bowl and grind
   20 sec/speed 10.

2. Add butter, eggs and 150 g lemon juice and cook
   20 min/90°C/speed 2 without measuring cup.

3. Insert measuring cup and mix **25 sec/speed 6**. Transfer into
   2 sterilised jam jars with twist-off lids and close immediately.
   Allow to cool before serving or storing in the refrigerator.

TIPS

• Lemon curd keeps in the refrigerator for up to one month.

• Serve as a spread on toast or scones, as a filling for cakes and tarts, or as a dessert,
  mixed with an equal amount of softly whipped cream and served with biscuits.

 10 min   1 h 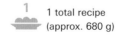 easy  1 total recipe (approx. 680 g)

Per jar:
Energy 8921 kJ/2135 kcal
Protein 21 g/Carbs 247 g/Fat 115 g

DESSERTS AND SWEETS

CUSTARD

INGREDIENTS

½-1 vanilla pod
500 g milk
2 egg yolks or 1 egg
50 g sugar
1 pinch salt
20-30 g cornflour (starch) (see tip)

USEFUL ITEMS

cling film

PREPARATION

1. Split vanilla pod lengthwise and scrape out seeds. Place seeds and vanilla pod into mixing bowl.
2. Add milk, egg yolks, sugar, salt and cornflour into mixing bowl and cook **7 min/90°C/🥄/speed 3**.
3. Transfer vanilla custard into a serving bowl or individual dessert bowls and remove vanilla pod. Serve lukewarm or cover with cling film in direct contact with the custard and store in refrigerator until ready to serve.

TIPS

- This is a thick custard. For a pouring custard, reduce cornflour to 10 g or use the Vanilla sauce (crème anglaise) recipe.
- Replace the vanilla pod with 10 g homemade vanilla sugar.

VARIATIONS

- **Vanilla custard with whisked egg whites:** when the custard is ready, transfer into a bowl, clean and dry mixing bowl thoroughly and **insert butterfly whisk**. Place 2 egg whites into mixing bowl and whisk **2 min/speed 3.5**. Fold whisked egg whites carefully with a spoon into the lukewarm custard. Cover and refrigerate until ready to serve.
- **Pastry cream (crème pâtissière):** Proceed as directed by the recipe, using 1 vanilla pod, 500 g whole milk, 2 eggs, 2 egg yolks, 80 g sugar and 50 g flour. For a richer flavour and smoother texture, after cooking in step 2 add 50 g cold unsalted butter and mix **10 sec/speed 4**.

 5 min
 15 min
 easy
4
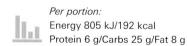 4 portions

Per portion:
Energy 805 kJ/192 kcal
Protein 6 g/Carbs 25 g/Fat 8 g

CHOCOLATE CUSTARD

INGREDIENTS

150 g dark chocolate (70% cocoa),
   cut into pieces (see tip)
500 g milk
100 g sugar
20 g cornflour (starch) (see tip)
2 eggs
1 tbsp butter or 1-2 tbsp cream
   (optional)

PREPARATION

1. Place chocolate into mixing bowl and grate **10 sec/speed 10**.
2. Add milk, sugar, cornflour and eggs and cook **12 min/90°C/speed 3**.
3. Add butter and mix **10 sec/speed 4**. Transfer immediately into individual dessert bowls and allow to cool. Refrigerate for at least one hour before serving.

TIPS

- Adjust amount of chocolate to your taste: 120 g for a milder flavour, 180 g for a rich chocolate dessert.
- If using chocolate with a lower cocoa percentage, decrease sugar amount as desired.
- For a pouring custard, omit cornflour.

 5 min 1 h 20 min easy 6 6 portions

 *Per portion:*
Energy 1844 kJ/441 kcal
Protein 10 g/Carbs 48 g/Fat 23 g

CRÈME CARAMEL (FLAN)

INGREDIENTS

500 g whole milk
4 eggs
130 g sugar (caster sugar)
200 g liquid caramel (see tip)
700 g water

USEFUL ITEMS

6 ceramic soufflé dishes
    (approx. Ø 8 cm, height 4.5 cm)
aluminium foil or heatproof
    cling film
toothpick

PREPARATION

1. Place whole milk, eggs and sugar into mixing bowl and mix **10 sec/speed 4**.
2. Pour approx. 2 tbsp liquid caramel into each of 6 ceramic soufflé dishes (Ø 8 cm, height 4.5 cm), covering the base. Fill dishes with egg mixture and cover with aluminium foil or heatproof cling film. Place 4 dishes into Varoma dish and 2 onto Varoma tray.
3. Place water into mixing bowl, place Varoma into position and steam **30 min/Varoma/speed 1**. Carefully remove aluminium foil or cling film and insert a toothpick to test if done. If toothpick does not come out clean, steam a further **5-10 min/Varoma/speed 1**.
4. Allow to cool 1 hour before placing in refrigerator. Chill for a minimum of 1 hour. Tip each crème caramel upside down onto a plate and carefully remove soufflé dish. Serve immediately.

TIPS
- Chilling crème caramel overnight gives it more time to set. The firmer the crème caramel, the easier it is to unmould.
- To make your own liquid caramel, melt 200 g sugar with 2 tbsp water and 2 tsp lemon juice in a medium-size, very clean saucepan over medium-high heat. Do not stir, but occasionally swirl the saucepan, until sugar becomes a fairly dark amber. At this point, **very carefully** pour in approx. 100 g hot water (it will bubble up and spatter). Stir over medium heat until all caramel is dissolved and syrup thickens slightly. This syrup will keep for weeks refrigerated in a sealed jar.

VARIATION
- Instead of individual portions, make one large rectangular crème caramel using a 1 litre rectangular dish (22 cm x 12 cm x 7 cm). Cover with aluminium foil, place into Varoma dish and steam **40 min/Varoma/speed 1**.

 15 min   2 h 45 min   easy   6 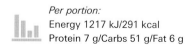 6 portions

Per portion:
Energy 1217 kJ/291 kcal
Protein 7 g/Carbs 51 g/Fat 6 g

FLOATING ISLANDS

INGREDIENTS

Vanilla sauce (crème anglaise)
450 g milk
6 egg yolks
70 g sugar
15 g vanilla sugar, homemade

Meringue islands
30 g sugar
6 egg whites
1 pinch salt
30 g liquid caramel (see tips)
    (optional)
25 g pistachio nuts, unsalted,
    chopped (optional)

PREPARATION

Vanilla sauce (crème anglaise)

1. Place milk, egg yolks, sugar and vanilla sugar into mixing bowl and heat **7 min/80°C/speed 4**, then mix **5 sec/speed 5**. Transfer into a serving bowl or into individual dessert bowls and allow to cool. Clean and dry mixing bowl thoroughly.

Meringue islands

2. Place sugar into mixing bowl and grind **10 sec/speed 10**.
3. **Insert butterfly whisk**. Add egg whites and salt and whisk **6 min/70°C/speed 3.5**.
4. Transfer egg whites in 6 portions onto Varoma tray and allow any liquid to drain for a few minutes. Transfer egg whites onto cool or lukewarm vanilla sauce. Just before serving, drizzle with liquid caramel and sprinkle with chopped pistachios.

TIPS
- Whisk the egg whites just before serving. The mixing bowl and butterfly whisk must be absolutely clean and free of any fatty residues.
- To make your own liquid caramel, see the tip in the Crème caramel recipe.

VARIATION
- Instead of caramel or chopped pistachios, sprinkle with any chopped nuts, preferably toasted, with crushed praline, or with chocolate flakes.

Step 1

 15 min   40 min   easy   6 portions

 Per portion:
Energy 887 kJ/212 kcal
Protein 10 g/Carbs 23 g/Fat 9 g

SABAYON (ZABAGLIONE)

INGREDIENTS

60 g dry Marsala wine

60 g dry white wine

120 g sugar (caster sugar)

6 egg yolks

PREPARATION

1. **Insert butterfly whisk.** Place Marsala wine, white wine, sugar and egg yolks into mixing bowl and heat **9 min/70°C/speed 3**. Serve immediately in glasses or in dessert bowls.

TIP

• Serve plain or as a sauce with fresh fruit, stewed fruit or apple strudel.

VARIATION

• Replace the Marsala and white wine combination with your favourite wine, or with grape juice for an alcohol-free dessert.

 5 min 15 min easy 4 portions

 *Per portion:* Energy 1047 kJ/250 kcal
Protein 5 g/Carbs 31 g/Fat 10 g

CHOCOLATE MOUSSE

INGREDIENTS

50 g sugar
200 g dark chocolate,
    min. 50% cocoa,
    cut into pieces
100 g cream, min. 30% fat
4 eggs, separated
1 pinch salt

PREPARATION

1. Place sugar into mixing bowl and grind **10 sec/speed 10**.
   Scrape down sides of mixing bowl with spatula.
2. Add dark chocolate and cream and melt **4 min/50°C/speed 2**.
3. Add egg yolks to mixing bowl and mix **15 sec/speed 4**.
   Transfer mixture into a medium size bowl and set aside.
   Clean and dry mixing bowl thoroughly.
4. **Insert butterfly whisk**. Place egg whites and salt into mixing bowl
   and whisk **3 min/speed 3.5** or until stiff. Add whisked egg whites
   to reserved chocolate mixture and carefully fold in using spatula.
   Pour into 6 individual dessert bowls and refrigerate for at least 3 hours
   before serving.

VARIATIONS
• For a darker mousse, use chocolate with 70% cocoa.
• Add 2-3 tsp orange-flavoured liqueur or rum in step 3.
• Fold in finely grated orange zest or chocolate chips in step 4,
  after folding in the egg whites.

 20 min   3 h 20 min   easy 6 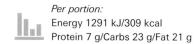 6 portions

Per portion:
Energy 1291 kJ/309 kcal
Protein 7 g/Carbs 23 g/Fat 21 g

BERRY MOUSSE

INGREDIENTS

5 gelatine sheets (2 g per sheet)
50 g water, plus extra for soaking
300 g mixed fresh red berries
  (e.g. strawberries, raspberries)
  or mixed frozen red berries
200 g sugar (caster sugar)
250 g curd cheese (quark) or ricotta
  cheese
250 g cream, min. 30% fat, chilled
fresh mint leaves, to garnish

PREPARATION

1. Soak gelatine sheets in a bowl of cold water for a few minutes or as per packet instructions.
2. Place water into mixing bowl and heat **2 min/60°C/speed 1**.
3. Drain gelatine sheets, add to mixing bowl and stir **5 sec/speed 2** until gelatine is completely dissolved.
4. Weigh 50 g berries into a bowl and reserve for garnish. Add remaining berries, sugar and curd cheese into mixing bowl and blend **20 sec/speed 8**. Transfer mixture into a large bowl and refrigerate until gelatine starts to set and mixture has the consistency of heavy cream (approx. 30 min). Clean and dry mixing bowl.
5. **Insert butterfly whisk**, add chilled cream and whip **speed 3** until cream has consistency of whipped cream, watching carefully to avoid over-whipping.
6. Gently fold whipped cream into fruit mixture with aid of spatula. Pour fruit mousse into 6 dessert bowls and refrigerate for 4 hours. Garnish with reserved fruit and with fresh mint leaves and serve chilled.

TIPS
• Serve fruit mousse with a berry coulis.
• Replace gelatine sheets with gelatine powder as follows: in step 1, place 20 g gelatine powder and 50 g water into mixing bowl. Allow to soak for 5 minutes or as per packet instructions, then dissolve **2 min/60°C/speed 3**. Proceed with step 4 as directed by the recipe.

VARIATION
• Curd cheese (quark) can also be replaced with cream cheese.

Step 1

 20 min   4 h 50 min   medium   6
 6 portions   *Per portion:*
Energy 1432 kJ/342 kcal
Protein 7 g/Carbs 38 g/Fat 18 g

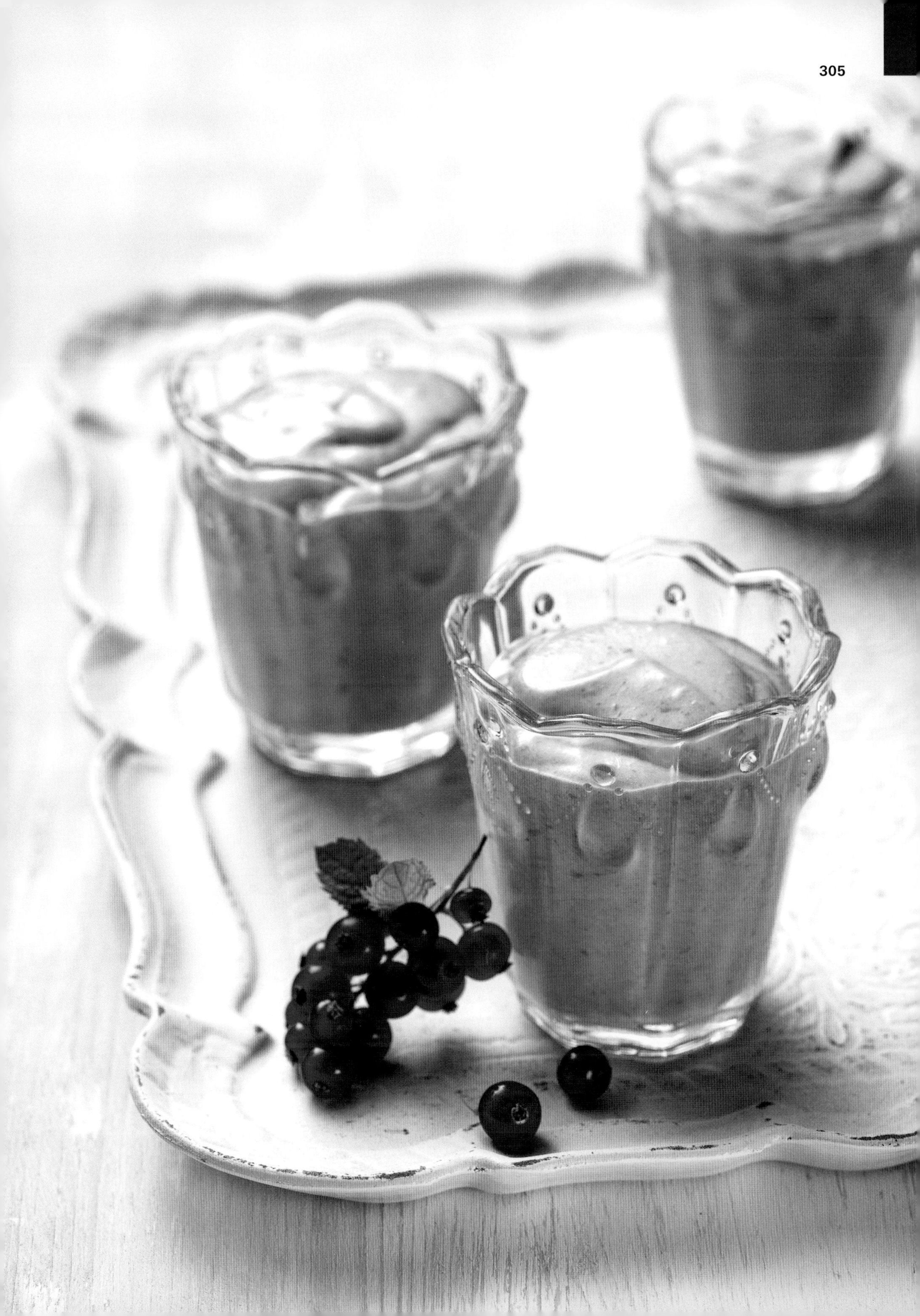

BERRY FOAM

INGREDIENTS

140 g sugar

500 g mixed frozen red berries

10-30 g lime juice or lemon juice

1 egg white

100 g mixed fresh red berries,
   to garnish

PREPARATION

1. Place sugar into mixing bowl and grind **15 sec/speed 10**.
2. Add mixed frozen red berries, lime juice and egg white into mixing bowl. Blend with aid of spatula **40 sec/speed 5**.
3. **Insert butterfly whisk** and whisk **3 min/speed 3.5**. Serve cold in dessert bowls, garnished with mixed fresh red berries.

 10 min   10 min   easy 8 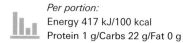 8 portions

Per portion:
Energy 417 kJ/100 kcal
Protein 1 g/Carbs 22 g/Fat 0 g

FROZEN FRUIT SORBET

INGREDIENTS

60-100 g sugar, to taste

500 g fruit, cut into pieces as needed, frozen in a single layer (see tip)

2 tsp lemon juice (optional)

1 egg white (see tip) (optional)

PREPARATION

1. Place sugar into mixing bowl and grind **10 sec/speed 10**.
2. Add frozen fruit, lemon juice and egg white and blend **1 min 30 sec/speed 5** with aid of spatula. Serve immediately.

TIPS

- Fruit should be frozen in individual pieces or small clusters. Cut fruit into pieces as needed, spread out on a tray, freeze, then use frozen fruit in recipe or transfer to a freezer bag for later use.
- For a firmer consistency, place the sorbet in the freezer for 15 minutes before serving.
- If using frozen berries, allow to rest at room temperature 10-15 minutes before step 2.
- For a lighter texture and flavour when using the egg white, after step 2 blend **30 sec/speed 10**.
- For a creamier sorbet: **insert butterfly whisk** after step 2 and whip **1 min/speed 3**.

VARIATIONS

- Replace lemon juice with 2 tsp homemade vanilla sugar.
- **Quick milkshake:** place 1-2 tbsp sorbet and 200 g milk into mixing bowl and mix **10 sec/speed 6**.

Tip

 5 min   5 min   easy   4 4 portions   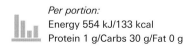 Per portion: Energy 554 kJ/133 kcal Protein 1 g/Carbs 30 g/Fat 0 g

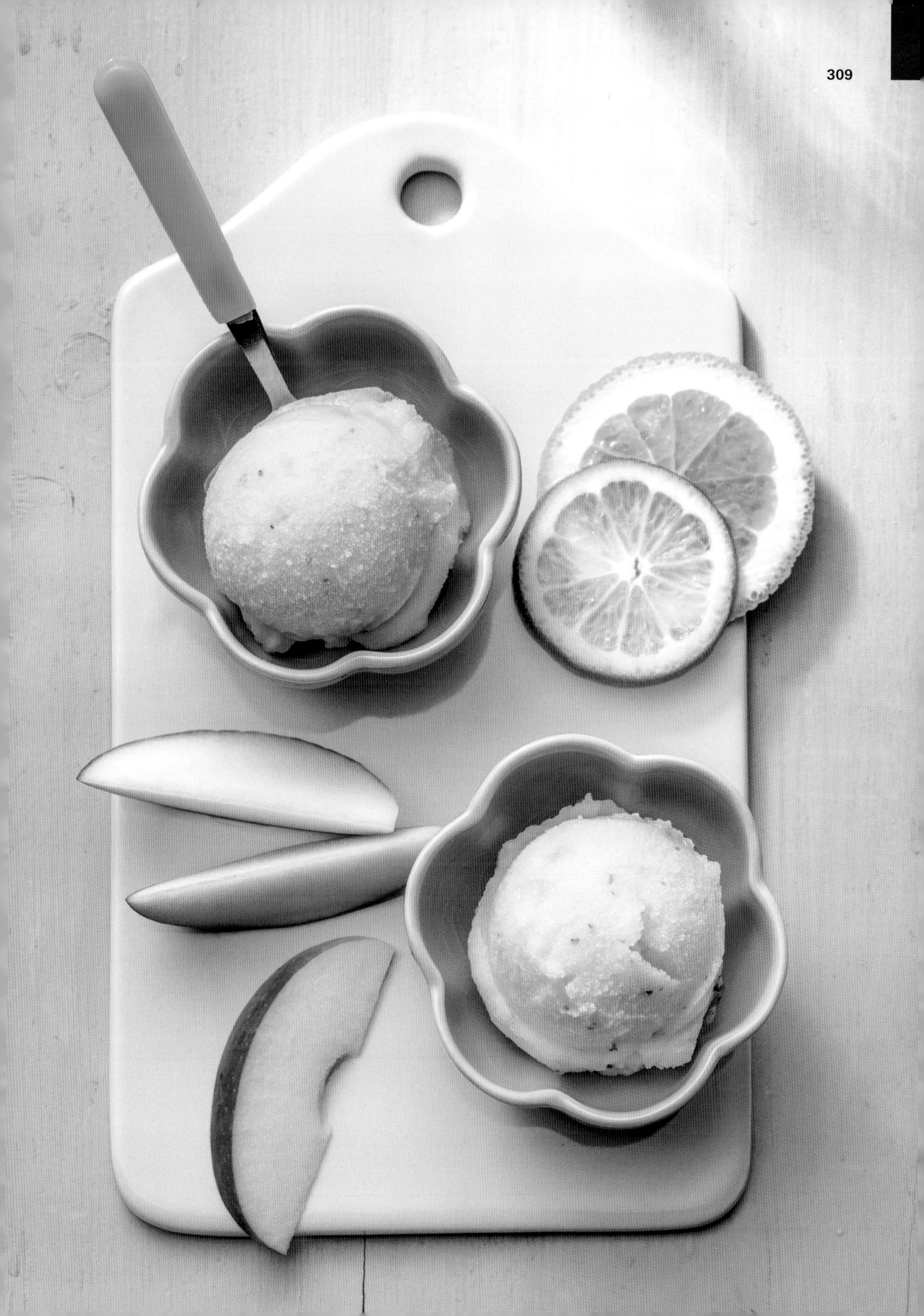

QUICK FRUIT SORBET

INGREDIENTS

180 g sugar

1 lemon, peeled, white pith and
    pips removed

300 g mixed fresh fruit,
    cut into pieces as needed

1000 g ice cubes

PREPARATION

1. Place sugar into mixing bowl and grind **15 sec/speed 10**.
2. Add lemon and mixed fresh fruit and chop **10 sec/speed 5**.
3. Add ice cubes and blend **1 min 30 sec/speed 9** with aid of spatula.
   Serve immediately.

TIPS
- For a creamier consistency, add one egg white in step 2.
- Instead of peeling the lemon you can squeeze out the juice and add it in step 2.

 10 min   10 min   easy   8 portions

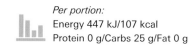
Per portion:
Energy 447 kJ/107 kcal
Protein 0 g/Carbs 25 g/Fat 0 g

LEMON SORBET

INGREDIENTS

650 g water
350 g sugar
200 g lemon juice (5-7 lemons),
    freshly squeezed
1 egg white

USEFUL ITEMS

freezable containers
    (e.g. plastic, silicone)
cling film

PREPARATION

1. Place 400 g water and sugar into mixing bowl and cook **5 min/100°C/speed 3**.
2. Add remaining 250 g water and lemon juice and mix **3 sec/speed 3**.
3. Add egg white and mix **3 sec/speed 4**. Pour mixture up to 4 cm high into freezable containers (e.g. plastic, silicone) and cover with cling film. Cool mixture completely before freezing for at least 8 hours.
4. Cut frozen mixture into pieces (approx. 4 cm x 4 cm) with a long sharp knife. Place pieces into mixing bowl and crush **30 sec/speed 9**, then mix **30 sec/speed 4** with aid of spatula. Serve immediately in dessert bowls.

 10 min   8 h 30 min   easy   8 portions   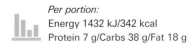 Per portion:
Energy 1432 kJ/342 kcal
Protein 7 g/Carbs 38 g/Fat 18 g

FRUIT ICE CREAM

INGREDIENTS

60 g sugar, adjust to taste
500 g frozen fruit, cut into pieces
    as needed, frozen in a single
    layer (see tip)
120 g cream

PREPARATION

1. Place sugar into mixing bowl and grind **15 sec/speed 10**.
2. Add frozen fruit and crush **15 sec/speed 8**.
3. Add cream and blend **40 sec/speed 5** with aid of spatula.
   Serve immediately.

TIPS

• For a firmer consistency, place the ice cream in the freezer for 15 minutes
  before serving.
• Whenever you have leftover fruit, freeze it for making ice cream later.
• Freeze fruit in individual pieces or small clusters. Cut fruit into pieces as needed,
  spread out on a tray in a single layer, freeze, then use frozen fruit in recipe or
  transfer to a freezer bag for later use.

VARIATIONS

• Use any frozen fruit (e.g. strawberries, raspberries, cherries, peaches).
• For a lighter version, replace cream with plain yoghurt or curd cheese (quark),
  or a combination of the two.

 5 min   5 min   easy   6 portions   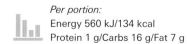 Per portion:
Energy 560 kJ/134 kcal
Protein 1 g/Carbs 16 g/Fat 7 g

VANILLA ICE CREAM

INGREDIENTS

2 vanilla pods
600 g whole milk
200 g cream, min. 30% fat
180 g sugar
6 egg yolks
1 pinch salt (optional)

USEFUL ITEMS

freezable containers
   (e.g. aluminium, silicone)
cling film

PREPARATION

1. Split vanilla pods lengthwise and scrape out seeds. Place vanilla seeds and pods into mixing bowl. Add whole milk, cream, sugar, egg yolks and salt, and cook **8 min/90°C/speed 2**. Remove vanilla pods.
2. Pour mixture, up to 4 cm high, into shallow freezable containers (e.g. aluminium, silicone) and cover with cling film. Allow mixture to cool completely before freezing for at least 10 hours.
3. Place frozen mixture into refrigerator for 15 minutes, then cut into pieces (4 cm x 4 cm) with a long sharp knife (see step photos in chocolate ice cream recipe). Place half the pieces into mixing bowl and crush **20 sec/speed 6**, then mix **10 sec/speed 4** with aid of spatula. Transfer ice cream into a bowl.
4. Place remaining frozen cream pieces into mixing bowl and crush **20 sec/speed 6**, then mix **10 sec/speed 4** with aid of spatula. Transfer into bowl with ice cream and serve immediately.

TIPS

- For a firmer consistency, place the ice cream in the freezer for 15 minutes before serving.
- Garnish with chopped pistachios, coconut flakes or chocolate drops.
- Top with whipped cream and chocolate or fruit sauce.

 15 min   12 h   medium   8   8 portions   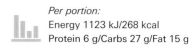 *Per portion:* Energy 1123 kJ/268 kcal Protein 6 g/Carbs 27 g/Fat 15 g

CHOCOLATE ICE CREAM

INGREDIENTS

100 g dark chocolate, 70% cocoa,
   cut into pieces
50 g cocoa powder
400 g whole milk
200 g cream, min. 30% fat
150 g sugar
4 egg yolks
1 pinch salt (optional)

USEFUL ITEMS

freezable containers
   (e. g. aluminium, silicone)
cling film

PREPARATION

1. Place dark chocolate into mixing bowl and chop **5 sec/speed 8**. Scrape down sides of mixing bowl with spatula.

2. Add cocoa powder, whole milk, cream, sugar, egg yolks and salt and cook **8 min/90°C/speed 2**. Pour mixture, up to 4 cm high, into shallow freezable containers (e.g. aluminium, silicone) and cover with cling film. Allow mixture to cool completely before freezing for at least 10 hours.

3. Place frozen mixture into refrigerator for 15 minutes, then cut into pieces (4 cm x 4 cm) with a long sharp knife. Place half the pieces into mixing bowl and crush **20 sec/speed 6**, then mix **10 sec/speed 4** with aid of spatula. Transfer ice cream into a bowl.

4. Place remaining frozen cream pieces into mixing bowl and crush **20 sec/speed 6**, then mix **10 sec/speed 4** with aid of spatula. Transfer into bowl with ice cream and serve immediately.

TIPS

- For a firmer consistency, place the ice cream in the freezer for 15 minutes before serving.
- Garnish with chopped pistachios, coconut flakes or chocolate drops.
- Top with whipped cream and chocolate or fruit sauce.

VARIATION

- For a spicy chocolate ice cream add some chilli powder in step 1.

 15 min   12 h   medium 8 8 portions   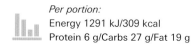 *Per portion:*
Energy 1291 kJ/309 kcal
Protein 6 g/Carbs 27 g/Fat 19 g

Step 2

Step 3

PROFITEROLES

INGREDIENTS

Choux pastry
150 g water
80 g butter, unsalted, cut into
    pieces
1 pinch salt
2 tsp sugar (10 g)
120 g flour
3 eggs (53-63 g each)

Chocolate sauce and assembly
250 g dark chocolate, 70% cocoa,
    cut into pieces
40 g butter, unsalted, cut into
    pieces
200 g milk
vanilla ice cream, homemade
    or ready-made

USEFUL ITEMS

baking tray and paper
icing bag and Ø 10 mm nozzle
ice cream scoop

PREPARATION

Choux pastry

1. Place water, butter, salt and sugar into mixing bowl and heat
   5 min/100°C/speed 1.
2. Add flour and mix **20 sec/speed 4**. Remove mixing bowl and set
   aside to cool for 10 minutes.
3. Preheat oven to 200°C. Line a baking tray with baking paper and
   set aside.
4. Place mixing bowl back into position and mix **speed 5**, adding eggs
   one at a time through hole in mixing bowl lid onto rotating blades.
   After adding the last egg mix a further **30 sec/speed 5**.
5. Place pastry mixture into an icing bag and pipe balls (walnut-size)
   onto prepared baking tray, leaving a 5 cm space between them.
   Bake for 20-25 minutes (200°C) or until golden brown. Turn off oven
   and open oven door slightly, leaving it ajar for 10 minutes to allow
   pastry to dry. Remove tray from oven and allow choux pastries to cool
   completely.

Chocolate sauce and assembly

6. Place dark chocolate into mixing bowl and chop **10 sec/speed 9**.
7. Add butter and milk and heat **4 min/100°C/speed 2**. Transfer into
   a bowl and set aside.
8. Cut cold choux pastries into halves. Place one scoop of ice cream onto
   each bottom half and cover with top half. Serve 2-3 choux pastries per
   person with chocolate sauce drizzled on top.

TIPS
- If you don't have an icing bag, cut the corner off a sturdy freezer bag and use as
  directed to pipe choux pastries onto baking tray.
- Use a wet finger to flatten any bumps on choux pastries before baking.
- If you prepare your own ice cream, take it out of the freezer and mix it in a clean
  mixing bowl to soften it before using in step 8.
- Profiteroles can be prepared in advance: fill choux pastries with ice cream and store
  in the freezer. Prepare and pour the chocolate sauce just before serving.

---

 20 min   2 h   medium   18
18 pieces

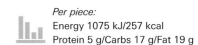
Per piece:
Energy 1075 kJ/257 kcal
Protein 5 g/Carbs 17 g/Fat 19 g

Step 2

Step 4

Step 5

Tip

TIRAMISÙ

INGREDIENTS
2 eggs
1 egg yolk
130 g sugar (caster sugar)
500 g mascarpone
300 g sponge fingers
400 g strong brewed coffee, chilled
20 g cocoa powder, unsweetened

USEFUL ITEMS
rectangular dish
    (30 cm x 20 cm x 6 cm)
cling film

PREPARATION
1. **Insert butterfly whisk**. Place eggs, egg yolk and sugar into mixing bowl and whip **6 min/speed 4**. **Remove butterfly whisk.**
2. Mix **2 min/speed 3** while adding mascarpone in spoonfuls through hole in mixing bowl lid onto rotating blades.
3. Briefly soak sponge fingers in chilled coffee until they soak up just enough liquid without falling apart. Arrange half of the soaked sponge fingers in the bottom of a rectangular dish (30 cm x 20 cm x 6 cm). Spread half of the mascarpone mixture over the sponge fingers base. Cover with remaining soaked sponge fingers, and spread remaining mascarpone mixture on top. Cover with cling film and refrigerate for 5 hours. Dust with cocoa powder just before serving.

TIP
• This dessert can be frozen. Allow to thaw at least five hours in the refrigerator before serving.

VARIATION
• Replace 50 g of the coffee with 50 g liqueur or brandy (e.g. almond liqueur, Cognac, rum).

Step 3

 15 min   5 h 20 min   easy   8 portions

Per portion:
Energy 2081 kJ/497 kcal
Protein 10 g/Carbs 47 g/Fat 30 g

RICE PUDDING

INGREDIENTS

1000 g milk
50 g sugar, plus some extra
1 pinch salt
220 g white short-grain rice,
    for rice pudding

PREPARATION

1. Place milk, sugar and salt into mixing bowl and heat **8 min/100°C/speed 1** without measuring cup.
2. Add rice and cook **30 min/90°C/⟲/speed 1** without measuring cup. Transfer into a serving bowl and allow to rest for 15 minutes. Serve warm or cold.

TIPS
- Sprinkle with sugar, brown sugar or cinnamon sugar, or serve with maple syrup.
- Serve with a red berry sauce.

VARIATIONS
- **Chocolate rice pudding:** add 1-2 tbsp cocoa powder in step 2 and proceed as directed by the recipe.
- **Rich rice pudding:** after cooking in step 2, add 2 eggs, lightly whisked, 1 tsp homemade vanilla sugar, 1 pinch ground cinnamon and 1 pinch ground nutmeg (optional) and mix **1 min/⟲/speed 3**. Transfer into a serving bowl and allow to rest as directed by the recipe.

 5 min   1 h   easy   8 /  8 portions

Per portion:
Energy 869 kJ/208 kcal
Protein 6 g/Carbs 35 g/Fat 5 g

BAKING – SWEET

SPONGE CAKE

INGREDIENTS

butter, for greasing
4 eggs, (53-63 g each) (see tip)
100-120 g sugar (caster sugar),
   to taste
1 tsp vanilla sugar, homemade
   or ½ tsp natural vanilla extract
120 g plain flour
1 pinch salt (optional)

USEFUL ITEMS

springform tin (Ø 22 cm)
cooling rack

PREPARATION

1. Preheat oven to 180°C. Grease a springform tin (Ø 22 cm) and set aside.
2. **Insert butterfly whisk.** Place eggs, sugar and vanilla sugar into mixing bowl and whisk **6 min/37°C/speed 4.** Whisk for a further **6 min/speed 4.**
3. Add flour and salt around butterfly whisk and mix **4 sec/speed 3.**
4. **Remove butterfly whisk** and carefully complete stirring with spatula.
5. Transfer mixture into prepared springform tin and bake immediately for 20-25 minutes (180°C). Allow cake to cool approx. 10 minutes before removing from springform tin. Allow cake to cool completely on a cooling rack before slicing in half horizontally for filling.

TIPS

- This cake can be used as a base for a variety of different cakes with fillings such as fruit, flavoured cream or whipped cream (e.g. San Marcos cake, truffle cake, fraisier). Or serve it on its own or with a dusting of icing sugar.
- If eggs are small (closer to 53 g than to 63 g), use 5 eggs instead of 4, lightly whisk them in a bowl and measure 240 g eggs into the mixing bowl in step 2.
- If springform tin is larger, or if you wish to cut the cake into three layers, increase recipe using 1.5 x the ingredients, and increase baking time by a few minutes.
- Sugar has an impact on the cake's texture. For a very light and fluffy texture use 120 g sugar.
- Cake texture is at its best when consumed within one day. To prevent sponge cake from drying out, store it in a container in the refrigerator. Sponge cake will keep for 4-5 days in the refrigerator or up to 1 month in the freezer.

VARIATIONS

- **Chocolate sponge cake:** use only 80 g flour and add 40 g cocoa powder.
- **Rolled cake:** bake the sponge cake in a thin rectangular layer for use in jam rolls, Swiss rolls, etc. Transfer cake batter onto a baking tray lined with baking paper or a silicone mat. Spread batter into a rectangle (40 x 30 cm) and bake immediately for 8 minutes (180°C). Roll cake while it is still hot with the help of a clean kitchen towel. Allow to cool, carefully unroll, remove towel, spread filling and roll again.

 15 min   1 h 50 min   easy 8  8 slices

Per slice:
Energy 641 kJ/153 kcal
Protein 5 g/Carbs 26 g/Fat 3 g

Variation: rolled cake

YOGHURT CAKE

INGREDIENTS

80 g sunflower oil, plus extra
    for greasing
1 lemon, preferably organic,
    zest only
150 g sugar
3 eggs
200 g flour
120 g yoghurt, 10% fat
1 pinch salt
1 tbsp baking powder (15 g)
30 g icing sugar, for dusting

USEFUL ITEMS

bundt cake tin (Ø 22-24 cm)

PREPARATION

1. Preheat oven to 180°C. Grease a bundt cake tin (Ø 22-24 cm) and
   set aside.
2. Place lemon zest and sugar into mixing bowl and grind
   10 sec/speed 10. Scrape down sides of mixing bowl with spatula.
3. Add eggs and mix **30 sec/speed 3**.
4. Add flour, yoghurt, sunflower oil and salt and mix **1 min/speed 5**.
5. Add baking powder and mix **15 sec/speed 5**. Place mixture into
   prepared cake tin and bake for 30 minutes (180°C). Allow to cool in
   cake tin for approx. 10 minutes before transferring to a serving plate
   and leaving to cool completely. Dust with icing sugar and serve.

VARIATION
• Use different yoghurt flavours (e.g. coffee, vanilla, berry).

 10 min   1 h 40 min   easy   10 10 slices    *Per slice:* Energy 1075 kJ/257 kcal Protein 4 g/Carbs 34 g/Fat 11 g

LEMON CAKE

INGREDIENTS

170 g sunflower oil, plus extra for
    greasing
260 g flour, plus extra for dusting
300 g sugar
2-3 lemons, preferably organic,
    zest and juice
70 g cornflour (starch) or
    potato starch
4 eggs
170 g milk
1 tbsp baking powder (15 g)
30 g icing sugar, for dusting

USEFUL ITEMS

bundt cake tin (Ø 22-24 cm)

PREPARATION

1. Preheat oven to 180°C. Grease and flour a bundt cake tin (Ø 22-24 cm)
   and set aside.
2. Place sugar and zest of 2 lemons into mixing bowl and grind
   10 sec/speed 10.
3. Add flour, cornflour, sunflower oil, 80 g lemon juice, eggs, milk and
   baking powder and mix **30 sec/speed 5**. Transfer mixture into
   prepared bundt cake tin.
4. Bake for 35-45 minutes (180°C) or until golden. Allow to cool in
   cake tin for approx. 10 minutes before transferring to a serving plate
   and leaving to cool completely. Dust with icing sugar and serve.

VARIATIONS
• Replace lemons with 2 medium oranges (approx. 150 g each), for a total of
  approx. 20 g zest and 110 g juice.
• The cake can also be baked in a loaf tin (25 cm).

 15 min   2 h   easy   12 slices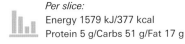
Per slice:
Energy 1579 kJ/377 kcal
Protein 5 g/Carbs 51 g/Fat 17 g

MARBLE CAKE

INGREDIENTS

300 g butter, unsalted, cut into
     pieces, plus extra for greasing
370 g flour, plus extra for dusting
280 g sugar
1 tsp vanilla sugar, homemade or
     ½ tsp natural vanilla extract
1 pinch salt
5 eggs
1 tbsp baking powder (15 g)
70 g milk
30 g cocoa powder

USEFUL ITEMS

bundt cake tin (Ø 22-24 cm)

PREPARATION

1. Preheat oven to 180°C. Grease and flour a bundt cake tin (Ø 22-24 cm) and set aside.
2. Place butter into mixing bowl and mix **40 sec/speed 5**.
3. Add 250 g sugar, vanilla sugar, salt, eggs, flour, baking powder and 40 g milk into mixing bowl and mix **40 sec/speed 5** with aid of spatula. Transfer half of cake mixture into prepared bundt cake tin, leaving remainder in mixing bowl.
4. Add cocoa powder, remaining 30 g sugar and remaining 30 g milk into mixing bowl and mix **5 sec/speed 5**. Scrape down sides of mixing bowl with spatula.
5. Mix a further **5 sec/speed 5**.
6. Layer cocoa cake mixture into bundt cake tin. To create a marble pattern, swirl through both layers with a fork. Bake for 50-60 minutes (180°C). Allow cake to cool in tin for approx. 15 minutes before transferring to a serving plate and leaving to cool completely. Cut into slices and serve.

TIPS
• If butter is very soft, omit step 2 and add the butter with the other ingredients in step 3.
• Dust with icing sugar or cover with a chocolate glaze.

VARIATIONS
• **Pound cake:** Omit cocoa marbling. Simply transfer all the cake mixture from step 3 into prepared bundt cake tin and bake for 50-60 min (180°C) as described in step 6.
• Flavour the cocoa mixture with ½ tsp rum essence, or with 20 g rum. If using rum, reduce milk to 10 g in step 3.

 10 min   2 h   medium 16 16 slices 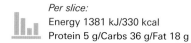 Per slice:
Energy 1381 kJ/330 kcal
Protein 5 g/Carbs 36 g/Fat 18 g

Step 5

CHOCOLATE CAKE

IINGREDIENTS

150 g butter, unsalted, cut into
    pieces, plus extra for greasing
6 eggs, separated
1 pinch salt
200 g sugar
250 g dark chocolate, cut into
    small pieces
50 g flour

USEFUL ITEMS

springform tin (Ø 22 cm)

PREPARATION

1. Preheat oven to 200°C. Grease a springform tin (Ø 22 cm) and set aside.
2. **Insert butterfly whisk.** Place egg whites and salt into mixing bowl and whisk **6 min/speed 3.5** or until stiff.
3. Add 20 g sugar and mix **20 sec/speed 3.5**. **Remove butterfly whisk.** Transfer into a bowl and set aside.
4. Place remaining 180 g sugar, egg yolks and butter into mixing bowl and mix **6 min/70°C/speed 4**.
5. Add dark chocolate, wait a few seconds for chocolate to soften and then mix **20 sec/speed 5**.
6. Add flour and mix **10 sec/speed 5**.
7. **Insert butterfly whisk.** Add reserved whisked egg whites and mix **15 sec/speed 2.5**. Transfer cake batter into prepared springform tin.
8. Bake for 10-15 minutes (200°C). Allow cake to cool for 5 minutes in the tin and serve warm or cold.

TIPS
- If using chocolate with 70% cocoa or more, reduce amount to 200 g.
- The mixing method and short baking time produce a mousse-like centre. If you prefer a firm cake, bake for 20-25 minutes (180°C).
- The cake can be served warm with vanilla ice cream.

VARIATION
- **Quick chocolate cake:** place chocolate into mixing bowl and grate **5 sec/speed 7**. Add butter and melt **4 min/60°C/speed 2**. Add flour, sugar, salt and eggs and mix **15 sec/speed 5**. Transfer into prepared springform tin and bake for approx. 20 minutes (180°C).

 15 min 40 min medium 12 slices

Per slice:
Energy 1334 kJ/319 kcal
Protein 5 g/Carbs 30 g/Fat 20 g

BROWNIES

INGREDIENTS

220 g butter, unsalted, cut into
    pieces, plus extra for greasing
250 g dark chocolate (70% cocoa),
    cut into pieces
380 g sugar
6 eggs
1 pinch salt
150 g flour
150 g halved walnuts (optional)

USEFUL ITEMS

cake tin (approx. 30 cm x 20 cm)
baking paper
toothpick or skewer

PREPARATION

1. Preheat oven to 170°C. Grease a cake tin (approx. 30 cm x 20 cm) and line with baking paper, letting edges of paper hang over sides of tin (the excess baking paper will serve as handles to lift out the brownies).
2. Place chocolate into mixing bowl and chop **5 sec/speed 7**.
3. Add butter and melt **4 min/70°C/speed 2**.
4. Add sugar, eggs, salt and flour and mix **1 min/speed 4**. Scrape down sides of mixing bowl with spatula.
5. Add walnuts and mix **10 sec/speed 4**.
6. Transfer into prepared cake tin, distributing batter evenly. Bake for 23-25 minutes (170°C), or until a toothpick or skewer inserted in the centre comes out with a few damp crumbs. Remove from cake tin using the baking paper to lift out the brownies. Allow to cool and serve brownies cut into squares.

TIPS

• If using chocolate with a lower cocoa percentage, increase chocolate and decrease sugar amount. For instance, for chocolate with 50% cocoa, increase chocolate to 360 g and decrease sugar to 260 g.

 10 min   50 min   easy   24
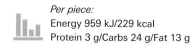 24 pieces   Per piece:
Energy 959 kJ/229 kcal
Protein 3 g/Carbs 24 g/Fat 13 g

CHOCOLATE CHIP MUFFINS

INGREDIENTS

150 g butter, unsalted, cut into
    pieces, plus extra for greasing
100 g dark chocolate,
    cut into pieces
2 eggs
200 g sugar
300 g flour
1 pinch salt
300 g milk
2 tsp baking powder (10 g)

USEFUL ITEMS

muffin tray

PREPARATION

1. Preheat oven to 180°C. Grease a muffin tray and set aside.
2. Place dark chocolate into mixing bowl and chop **6-10 sec/speed 5**. Transfer into a bowl and set aside.
3. Place butter, eggs, sugar, flour, salt, milk and baking powder into mixing bowl and mix **30 sec/speed 5**.
4. Add reserved chopped chocolate and mix **15 sec/☙/speed 4**. Transfer batter into prepared muffin tray. Bake muffins for 30 minutes (180°C) or until golden brown. Allow muffins to cool for 10 minutes before removing from muffin tray. Serve warm or cold.

TIP

• If you don't have a muffin tray, stack groups of 3 muffin liners together on a baking tray to serve as muffin moulds.

VARIATIONS

• **Double chocolate muffins:** insert a piece of chocolate into the centre of each muffin before baking.
• **Blueberry muffins:** omit step 2. Instead of chocolate, in step 4 add blueberries (approx. 150 g), either fresh or frozen, and stir **10 sec/☙/speed 1**. You can also fold the blueberries in with the spatula.

Step 1

Step 4

 15 min   1 h   easy   12 12 pieces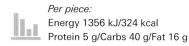
Per piece:
Energy 1356 kJ/324 kcal
Protein 5 g/Carbs 40 g/Fat 16 g

APPLE CAKE

INGREDIENTS

130 g butter, unsalted, softened,
cut into pieces, plus extra for
greasing
3-4 apples, tart (approx. 180 g each)
3 eggs
150 g sugar
30 g brandy (optional)
200 g flour
1 tbsp baking powder (15 g)
1 pinch salt
icing sugar, for dusting

USEFUL ITEMS

round cake tin (Ø 26-28 cm)
wooden skewer

Step 2

PREPARATION

1. Preheat oven to 180°C. Grease a round cake tin (Ø 26-28 cm) and set aside.
2. Peel apples, cut into quarters and remove core and seeds. With a sharp knife, make parallel incisions on the outside of the apple, cutting down but taking care not to cut completely through. Set apple quarters aside.
3. Place butter, eggs, sugar, brandy, flour, baking powder and salt into mixing bowl and mix **20 sec/speed 6**. Pour mixture into cake tin and spread evenly with spatula. Place reserved apple quarters on top, one next to the other, with incisions facing up.
4. Bake for 30-40 minutes (180°C) or until a skewer inserted into centre of cake comes out clean. Allow cake to cool in tin for approx. 10 minutes before transferring to a serving plate. Dust top of cake with icing sugar before serving.

TIPS
- You can leave the apples unpeeled.
- If a smaller Ø tin is used, increase baking time (e. g. 40-45 minutes for a Ø 24 cm tin). Fewer apples will be necessary for topping the smaller surface of the cake.

VARIATIONS
- Apples can be replaced with pears (prepared as directed for the apples), plums (halved, stones removed), peaches (halved, stones removed, and prepared as directed for the apples), apricots (halved, stones removed), or any other fruit to your taste. The amount of fruit pieces depends on the size of the cake. You need enough to distribute evenly over the surface of the cake.
- Brandy can be replaced with rum.

 20 min 1 h easy 8 8 slices

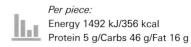 *Per piece:* Energy 1492 kJ/356 kcal Protein 5 g/Carbs 46 g/Fat 16 g

APPLE TART

INGREDIENTS

Pastry

75 g butter, unsalted, cut into
    pieces, plus extra for greasing
150 g flour, plus extra for dusting
1 pinch salt
½ tsp vanilla sugar, homemade or
    ¼ tsp natural vanilla extract
50 g water

Topping

900-1000 g apples (e. g. Reinette,
    Granny Smith, Braeburn,
    Pink Lady, Pippin, Gravenstein)
30 g sugar
10 g butter

USEFUL ITEMS

tart tin (Ø 26 cm)
rolling pin

PREPARATION

Pastry

1. Preheat oven to 200°C. Grease and flour a tart tin (Ø 26 cm) and set aside.
2. Place butter, flour, salt, vanilla sugar and water into mixing bowl and mix **20 sec/speed 4/⟲**.
3. Using a rolling pin, roll out pastry on a lightly floured surface. Line prepared tart tin with the pastry and set aside.

Topping

4. Peel apples, cut into quarters and remove core and pips. Cut apple quarters into thin slices and arrange in a fan pattern on top of pastry. Sprinkle with sugar and dot with small pieces of butter. Bake for 30-35 minutes (200°C) or until apples are golden. Serve warm or cold.

VARIATIONS

- Add a layer of apple compote on top of pastry before arranging apple slices.
- Sprinkle tart with ground cinnamon or ground hazelnuts before baking.
- Give the tart a little shine: brush it after baking with 2 tbsp heated apple jelly.

Step 1

Step 2

Step 4

 30 min   1 h   easy 8 / 8 slices

Per slice:
Energy 915 kJ/218 kcal
Protein 2 g/Carbs 30 g/Fat 10 g

APPLE STRUDEL

INGREDIENTS

Strudel pastry
370 g flour, plus extra for dusting
1 egg
70 g sunflower oil
120 g water
1 tsp white wine vinegar
½ tsp salt

Apple filling
100 g hazelnuts
130 g butter, unsalted, cut into
    pieces
80 g breadcrumbs
1 tsp ground cinnamon
100 g sugar
1 tbsp vanilla sugar, homemade or
    1½ tsp natural vanilla extract
20 g lemon juice
20 g rum (optional)
750 g apples, peeled
80 g raisins
icing sugar, for dusting

USEFUL ITEMS
cling film
baking tray (approx. 40 cm x 35 cm)
baking paper
rolling pin
2 large kitchen towels
    (approx. 80 cm x 45 cm)
scissors
pastry brush

PREPARATION

Strudel pastry
1. Place flour, egg, 40 g sunflower oil, water, white wine vinegar and salt into mixing bowl and knead **2 min/⚕**. Place dough on a lightly floured surface and form dough into a loaf shape. Brush with remaining sunflower oil, cover with cling film and let rest at room temperature for 30 minutes. Meanwhile, prepare filling.

Apple filling
2. Place hazelnuts into mixing bowl and chop **10 sec/speed 7**. Transfer into a bowl and set aside.
3. Place 40 g butter into mixing bowl and melt **2 min/70°C/speed 2**.
4. Add breadcrumbs and ½ tsp cinnamon and toast **6 min/Varoma/speed 2**.
5. Add chopped hazelnuts and mix **5 sec/speed 4**. Transfer into a bowl and set aside.
6. Place sugar, remaining ½ tsp cinnamon, vanilla sugar, lemon juice and rum into mixing bowl and mix **15 sec/↺/speed 4**.
7. Cut apples into quarters, remove cores, then cut quarters into slices. Add apples and raisins to mixing bowl and mix **5-10 sec/↺/speed 3** with aid of spatula, adjusting time according to desired size of apple pieces. Transfer into a bowl and set aside.
8. Place remaining 90 g butter into mixing bowl, melt **3 min/70°C/speed 1** and set aside for brushing.

Continued on page **344** ▶

 45 min   1 h 45 min   advanced   12 12 portions   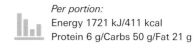 *Per portion:* Energy 1721 kJ/411 kcal Protein 6 g/Carbs 50 g/Fat 21 g

▶ Apple strudel, continued

Strudel assembly

9. Preheat oven to 190°C and line a large baking tray (approx. 40 cm x 35 cm) with baking paper.

10. Place a large kitchen towel (approx. 80 cm x 45 cm) onto a table and dust it with flour. Place dough onto kitchen towel, dust with flour and using a rolling pin, roll it out on the kitchen towel into a thin, rectangular shape. Cover with second kitchen towel and let it rest for 5 minutes.

11. Remove the top kitchen towel and place it on the table, its long edge overlapping slightly with the long edge of the other kitchen towel, to create a large surface on which to stretch the dough. Brush dough with some melted butter, then lift over the backs of hands and gently stretch it with your knuckles toward the table edges. Move around the edge of the dough and keep stretching the dough slowly and carefully toward and finally over the table edges, until the dough is very large, thin and transparent. Use scissors to cut off thick edges of dough. If holes appear while stretching, pinch them together lightly; small holes will not be visible after rolling the strudel.

12. Brush entire dough surface with some more melted butter, sprinkle reserved breadcrumb and hazelnut mixture in a wide band along the shortest edge of the pastry, leaving a few cm of dough uncovered along the edge and top the crumb mixture with the apple filling, forming a narrower band than the breadcrumb mixture. Lift up cloth at filling edge, using it to flip the dough. Roll strudel by pulling the first kitchen towel upwards and continuing with the next kitchen towel until the whole strudel is rolled. Pinch ends of roll shut, cutting off unnecessary excess dough and tucking dough ends underneath roll. With the help of the remaining kitchen towel, carefully transfer strudel onto prepared baking tray, forming strudel into a horseshoe shape if necessary to make it fit.

13. Brush top with remaining melted butter. Bake for 25-30 minutes (190°C) or until crisp and golden. Allow to cool a little, dust with icing sugar and serve warm, cut into thick slices.

Step 1

Step 10

Step 11

Step 12

Step 13

TIPS
- Serve with vanilla sauce, vanilla ice cream or whipped cream.
- The breadcrumb and hazelnut mixture traps juices from the apples and keeps the strudel crust crisp. Instead of using both, you can use all breadcrumbs or all hazelnuts.
- Before placing apples onto breadcrumb mixture, check whether they have released a lot of juice. For a drier filling, discard part of the juice.
- Dough can be prepared a day or two in advance and stored in the refrigerator.
- Instead of two kitchen towels, use a large tablecloth to roll the strudel.

VARIATIONS
- For a faster version, use ready-made strudel dough.
- You can form two apple strudels instead of one large one: when placing filling on top of dough, leave empty a channel of a few cm in the middle of the row of apples. Roll the strudel as described in the recipe, then cut through the channel to form two strudels, pinching the ends of each strudel shut.

CHEESECAKE (UNBAKED)

INGREDIENTS

200 g plain biscuits
80 g butter, unsalted, softened
250 g water
90 g jelly dessert powder,
    sweetened, lemon flavour
    (for 500 g liquid) (see tip)
400 g cream cheese
200 g cream
40 g sugar (caster sugar)

Jam topping

200 g jam, (e.g. strawberry,
    raspberry, plum)
2 tbsp lemon juice
1-2 tsp unflavoured gelatine
    powder (5 g) (see tip)
50 g water

USEFUL ITEMS

springform tin (Ø 24-26 cm)

PREPARATION

1. Place biscuits into mixing bowl and crush **5 sec/speed 10**.
2. Add butter and mix **5 sec/speed 5**.
3. Spread mixture into base of a non-stick springform tin (Ø 24-26 cm).
   Use a spoon or your hands to press crumb mixture down firmly
   to make a compact layer. Place springform tin in the freezer. Clean
   mixing bowl.
4. Place water into mixing bowl and heat **5 min/100°C/speed 1**.
5. Add lemon-flavoured jelly dessert powder, cream cheese, cream and
   sugar and mix **20 sec/speed 5**.
6. Remove springform tin from the freezer and transfer contents of
   mixing bowl into springform tin. Chill in refrigerator until filling is set
   (approx. 4 hours). Clean mixing bowl.

Jam topping

7. Place jam, lemon juice, unflavoured gelatine powder and water into
   mixing bowl and heat **3 min/80°C/speed 2**.
8. Allow mixture to cool for 10 minutes then pour it over the set
   cheesecake. Again chill cheesecake in refrigerator, for at least one
   hour. Serve cold.

TIPS

- Jelly dessert powder contains gelatine powder, sugar and flavourings. To replace
  90 g lemon-flavoured jelly dessert powder, use 10 g unflavoured gelatine powder,
  80 g sugar and 1 grated lemon zest.
- To replace gelatine powder (not jelly dessert powder) with gelatine sheets, use same
  weight of gelatine and soak sheets in cold water for five minutes. Drain, squeeze
  out water, discard soaking water and add gelatine to mixture.

 20 min
 5 h 30 min
 easy
8
8 slices

Per portion:
Energy 2351 kJ/562 kcal
Protein 10 g/Carbs 52 g/Fat 35 g

CHEESECAKE (BAKED)

INGREDIENTS

Base

120 g butter, unsalted, cut into
　　pieces, plus extra for greasing
250 g plain biscuits or digestive
　　biscuits
30 g brown sugar

Filling

750 g cream cheese
120 g cream, min. 30% fat
220 g sugar
1½ tsp vanilla sugar, homemade,
　　or natural vanilla extract
3 eggs
1 egg yolk

USEFUL ITEMS

springform tin (Ø 20 cm)
baking tray

PREPARATION

Base

1. Grease the bottom and sides of a springform tin (Ø 20 cm) generously with butter.
2. Place butter into mixing bowl and melt **2 min/100°C/speed 1**.
3. Add biscuits and sugar and crush **10 sec/speed 7**.
4. Spread crumb mixture into base of prepared springform tin. Use a spoon or your hands to press crumb mixture down firmly to make a compact layer. Refrigerate for 30 minutes.
5. Preheat oven to 220°C and clean mixing bowl.

Filling

6. Place cream cheese, cream, sugar and vanilla sugar into mixing bowl and mix **20 sec/speed 4**.
7. Add eggs and egg yolk and mix **20 sec/speed 4**. Pour cheesecake filling over crumb base.
8. Bake on a baking tray on the lowest shelf of oven for 10 minutes (220°C). Reduce temperature to 150°C and bake for a further 45-50 minutes or until mixture is almost set. Allow to cool for an hour in turned-off oven with door ajar. Allow to cool to room temperature, then cover and refrigerate for at least 4 hours before cutting into slices and serving.

TIP

- Cooling the cake slowly in the oven helps prevent surface cracks. If a crack does form, you can disguise it with one of the following: icing sugar, whipped cream, caramel sauce, chocolate sauce or fruit coulis.

VARIATIONS

- **Lime or lemon cheesecake:** in step 6, add the grated zest and juice of 2 limes or small lemons. Garnish cake with lime or lemon zest or wedges.
- **Raspberry swirl cheesecake:** after step 7, clean the mixing bowl. Place 150 g raspberries into mixing bowl and blend **30 sec/speed 10**. Pass purée through a fine sieve into a bowl. Stir 2 tbsp sugar into purée and drop purée onto unbaked cheesecake with a teaspoon. Swirl sauce into filling with a wooden skewer or a toothpick. Bake as directed by the recipe.

---

 15 min　　 7 h 20 min　　 medium　　 12 slices　　 Per slice:
Energy 3263 kJ/780 kcal
Protein 16 g/Carbs 59 g/Fat 53 g

Step 4

LEMON MERINGUE TART

INGREDIENTS

Pastry

100 g sugar
30 g almonds
200 g butter, unsalted, cut into
    pieces, plus extra for greasing
340 g flour
1 egg
1 pinch salt
1½ tsp vanilla sugar, homemade,
    or 1 tsp natural vanilla extract

Lemon filling

150 g sugar
3-5 lemons, preferably organic,
    zest and juice
1 egg
4 egg yolks
100 g butter, unsalted, cut into
    pieces

Meringue topping

160 g sugar
4 egg whites
1 pinch salt

USEFUL ITEMS

cling film
tart tin (Ø 24-26 cm)
rolling pin
baking paper
baking weights (e.g. dried beans)
cooling rack

PREPARATION

Pastry

1. Place sugar into mixing bowl and grind **15 sec/speed 10**.
2. Add almonds and grind **10 sec/speed 10**.
3. Add butter, flour, egg, salt and vanilla sugar into mixing bowl and mix **25-30 sec/speed 5** with aid of spatula. Remove pastry dough from mixing bowl, form into a flattened ball and wrap in cling film. Refrigerate for 1 hour.
4. Preheat oven to 180°C. Grease a tart tin and set aside.
5. Roll out half of the pastry (reserve the rest for another recipe or freeze) between 2 sheets of baking paper or cling film to a thickness of 4 mm, working quickly and handling the dough as little as possible to keep it chilled and easy to work with. Line prepared tart tin with dough and prick pastry with a fork to avoid air bubbles. Line pastry with baking paper and baking weights (e.g. dried beans) and blind-bake for 15 minutes (180°C). Remove baking paper and baking weights and bake for a further 5-10 minutes or until golden brown.

Lemon filling

6. Reduce oven temperature to 160°C.
7. Place sugar and zest of 1 lemon into mixing bowl and grind **20 sec/speed 10**.
8. Add egg, egg yolks and 130 g lemon juice and heat **12 min/70°C/speed 3**.
9. Add butter and mix **10 sec/speed 4**. Pour mixture into pastry case and distribute evenly with spatula. Bake for 10 minutes (160°C). Clean and dry mixing bowl thoroughly and proceed directly with next step, while tart is baking.

Continued on page **352** ▶

 25 min   2 h 30 min   advanced    8 slices plus extra pastry    *Per slice:* Energy 2178 kJ/521 kcal Protein 8 g/Carbs 62 g/Fat 27 g

► Lemon meringue tart, continued

Meringue topping

10. Place sugar into mixing bowl and grind **10 sec/speed 10**.

11. **Insert butterfly whisk.** Add egg whites and salt and whisk **5 min/50°C/speed 3.5** or until stiff. Spread meringue over hot lemon tart, creating swirls with a spoon or fork and making sure meringue touches all edges of the pastry, leaving no gap between filling and tart crust.

12. Bake for 10 minutes (160°C), or until meringue is lightly browned. Turn off oven and leave door ajar for 30 minutes to 1 hour to allow tart to cool gradually. Allow to cool a further 30 minutes on a cooling rack at room temperature. Serve either at room temperature or chilled.

TIPS

• For a nut-free pastry, omit almonds and use 370 g flour instead of 340 g.

• If the dough becomes warm and difficult to work with, place rolled out dough, still covered with sheets of baking paper or cling film, into refrigerator until dough is firm enough to handle.

• Refer to the Sweet shortcrust pastry recipe for an alternative method for rolling out the dough.

• For a crisp tart crust, make sure tart case is baked thoroughly (golden brown) before filling.

• Spreading the meringue over the hot filling and allowing it to cool gradually in the turned-off oven both help prevent the meringue from shrinking as it cools.

• Use extra pastry for another tart case or for biscuits (bake 10–12 minutes at 180°C, or until golden).

VARIATION

• **Lemon tart:** For a simple lemon tart, add an egg white to the filling in step 8 and omit the meringue topping.

Step 11

BUTTER BISCUITS

INGREDIENTS

250 g flour
100 g sugar, plus extra for dipping
100 g butter, unsalted, cut into
    pieces
1 egg
1 tsp baking powder

USEFUL ITEMS

baking tray and paper
cooling rack
air-tight container

Step 3

PREPARATION

1. Preheat oven to 180°C. Line a baking tray with baking paper and set aside.
2. Place flour, sugar, butter, egg and baking powder into mixing bowl and mix **20 sec/speed 6**.
3. Place some sugar onto a plate. Pinch together 1 tbsp dough and roll into a small ball (approx. Ø 3 cm). Dip the top in sugar, place onto prepared baking tray and flatten with a fork into a round biscuit shape. Repeat with remaining dough and bake 20 minutes (180°C) or until light golden. Allow to cool on a cooling rack before serving or storing in an air-tight container.

TIP
• In step 2, add natural flavours such as vanilla sugar, lemon zest, orange zest, ground cinnamon, or chopped candied ginger.

 20 min   50 min   easy   30 pieces 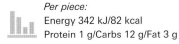 Per piece:
Energy 342 kJ/82 kcal
Protein 1 g/Carbs 12 g/Fat 3 g

CHOCOLATE CHIP COOKIES

INGREDIENTS

140 g dark chocolate,
    cut into pieces
130 g butter, unsalted, cut into
    pieces
100 g sugar
100 g brown sugar
1 egg
2 tsp vanilla sugar, homemade or
    1 tsp natural vanilla extract
180 g flour
½ tsp baking soda
½ tsp baking powder
1 pinch salt

USEFUL ITEMS

2 baking trays
baking paper
cooling rack
air-tight container

PREPARATION

1. Preheat oven to 180°C. Line two baking trays with baking paper and set aside.
2. Place dark chocolate into mixing bowl and chop **3-6 sec/speed 6**. Transfer into a bowl and set aside.
3. Place butter, sugar, brown sugar, egg and vanilla sugar into mixing bowl and mix **2 min/speed 3**.
4. Add flour, baking soda, baking powder and salt and mix **40 sec/speed 4**.
5. Add reserved chopped chocolate and stir **30 sec/speed 2**. Form dough with aid of 2 teaspoons into walnut-size balls and place them 5 cm apart onto prepared baking trays. Bake one baking tray after another for 10-12 minutes (180°C) until cookies are golden brown. Allow to cool on a cooling rack before serving or storing in an air-tight container.

VARIATION

• In step 5, add approx. 30 g chopped nuts or raisins in addition to chocolate.

Step 5

 20 min 50 min easy 30 30 pieces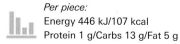

Per piece:
Energy 446 kJ/107 kcal
Protein 1 g/Carbs 13 g/Fat 5 g

DRINKS

LEMONADE

INGREDIENTS

2-3 lemons, preferably organic,
    unpeeled, cut into halves
1000 g water, chilled
100 g sugar (caster sugar),
    adjust to taste
10 ice cubes

PREPARATION

1. Place lemons, 500 g water and sugar into mixing bowl. Hold measuring cup in place and crush **2 sec/speed 10**.
2. Add remaining 500 g water. Insert simmering basket, hold it in place with spatula and strain lemonade into a jug. Add ice cubes and serve immediately.

TIPS
- Choose smaller lemons with smooth shiny peel, as these are juicier and have less white pith.
- For sweeter or tarter lemonade, adjust sugar to taste.

VARIATION
- Replace lemons with either 2 small oranges or 1 grapefruit, cut into quarters.

Step 2

 5 min   5 min   easy  6 glasses (200 ml each) 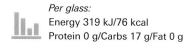 *Per glass:* Energy 319 kJ/76 kcal Protein 0 g/Carbs 17 g/Fat 0 g

LEMON SLUSH

INGREDIENTS

150 g sugar

lemon zest, from 1 lemon

4 lemons, peeled, white pith and
  pips removed

500 g water

500 g ice cubes

USEFUL ITEMS

straws

PREPARATION

1. Place sugar and lemon zest into mixing bowl and grind **30 sec/speed 10**.

2. Add lemons and water and blend **30 sec/speed 10**.

3. Add ice cubes and crush **20 sec/speed 6**. If large pieces of ice are still visible, crush a further **2 sec/speed 6**. Serve immediately with straws.

 10 min   10 min   easy  6 glasses (200 ml each)  *Per glass:* Energy 484 kJ/116 kcal Protein 0 g/Carbs 26 g/Fat 0 g

FRUIT NECTAR

INGREDIENTS

300 g mixed fresh fruit, cut into
  pieces as needed
1 lemon, peeled, white pith and
  pips removed
50 g sugar, adjust to taste
500 g water
ice cubes, to serve

PREPARATION

1. Place mixed fresh fruit, lemon and sugar into mixing bowl and blend **1 min/speed 9**.
2. Add water and mix **5 sec/speed 5**. Serve immediately with ice cubes.

TIPS
- If the peel of the fruit is edible, leave it on to enjoy all fibre and vitamins it contains.
- If the fruit is very ripe or sweet, the sugar can be omitted completely.
- Instead of peeling the lemon you can squeeze out the juice and add it in step 2.

VARIATION
- Make nectar with a single type of fruit or mix different types, for example:
  – 100 g orange, 100 g apple and 100 g pear
  – 200 g orange and 100 g mango
  – 100 g kiwi fruit and 200 g strawberries.

 10 min 10 min easy  5 glasses (200 ml each)  *Per glass:* Energy 324 kJ/77 kcal Protein 1 g/Carbs 17 g/Fat 0 g

SMOOTHIE

INGREDIENTS

350-450 g mixed fresh fruit,
 cut into pieces as needed
200-300 g fruit juice
 (e.g. apple, orange, grape,
 pineapple, cranberry)
50 g ice cubes
20-30 g lemon juice (optional)
1 tbsp sugar (optional)

PREPARATION

1. Place mixed fresh fruit, fruit juice, ice cubes, lemon juice and sugar into mixing bowl and chop **5 sec/speed 5**, then blend **1 min/speed 10**. Serve immediately.

TIPS
- For best results use ripe fruit. If fruit is lacking in flavour, add the optional sugar.
- Lemon juice helps keep colours bright and enhances the taste of the fruit.
- Fresh fruit can be replaced with frozen fruit. To freeze fruit, cut into pieces as needed, spread out on a tray in a single layer, freeze, then use frozen fruit in recipe or transfer to a freezer bag for later use.
- If using mostly frozen fruit, partially defrost fruit first, and omit ice cubes.
- If using very juicy fruit such as melon or watermelon, increase fruit weight to 500 g and reduce juice weight to 150 g.
- If using a large proportion of less juicy fruit such as bananas, reduce fruit weight to 350 g and increase juice to 300 g.

VARIATION
- Suggested combinations:
 – Melon, apple, orange juice
 – Peach, apple, banana, grape juice
 – Pear, banana, apple juice
 – Mango, raspberries, apple juice
 – Pineapple, plums, orange juice

 5 min 5 min easy  4 glasses (200 ml each) Per glass: Energy 344 kJ/82 kcal Protein 1 g/Carbs 18 g/Fat 0 g

GREEN SMOOTHIE

INGREDIENTS

150 g cucumbers, cut into pieces
60 g fresh spinach leaves
3 sprigs fresh parsley, leaves only
3 sprigs fresh mint, leaves only
1 lemon, peeled, white pith
    and pips removed
1 cm fresh ginger, cut in slices
    (2 mm)
¼ tsp sea salt (optional)
1 orange (approx. 100 g), peeled,
    white pith and pips removed
1 apple (approx. 100 g),
    cut into quarters
50-100 g ice cubes
50-100 g water or coconut water

PREPARATION

1. Place cucumbers, spinach leaves, parsley, mint, lemon, ginger, salt, orange, apple, ice cubes and water into mixing bowl and blend **1 min/speed 9**. Serve immediately.

TIP
• Adjust ingredient quantities according to your taste.

VARIATION
• Replace the fruit and vegetables in this recipe with any other varieties to create your own variation (e.g. pear, celery, grapes, kale, citrus fruit).

 10 min   10 min    easy   4 glasses (150 ml each)   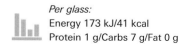 *Per glass:* Energy 173 kJ/41 kcal Protein 1 g/Carbs 7 g/Fat 0 g

STRAWBERRY MILKSHAKE

INGREDIENTS

300 g strawberries
300 g vanilla ice cream,
    cut into pieces
4 ice cubes (optional)
30 g sugar
370 g milk

PREPARATION

1. Place strawberries, vanilla ice cream, ice cubes, sugar and milk into mixing bowl and blend **1 min/speed 7**. Serve immediately in glasses with straws.

VARIATIONS

- Replace strawberries with any other fruit such as raspberries, apricots or bananas.
- **Coffee milkshake**: omit fruit, replace vanilla ice cream with coffee ice cream and add 1 tsp instant coffee.
- **Chocolate milkshake**: omit fruit, replace vanilla ice cream with chocolate ice cream and add 1 tbsp cocoa powder.

 5 min   5 min  easy 4 glasses (200 ml each)

 *Per glass:*
Energy 344 kJ/82 kcal
Protein 1 g/Carbs 18 g/Fat 0 g

HOT CHOCOLATE

INGREDIENTS

500 g milk
100-150 g chocolate,
    cut into pieces

PREPARATION

1. Place milk and chocolate into mixing bowl and heat
   6 min/80°C/speed 1. Pour into cups and serve immediately.

TIPS
- Serve with a pastry or biscuits.
- Top with whipped cream or frothed milk.
- Use dark or milk chocolate for this recipe. For chocolate with a high cocoa
  percentage (50-70%), add 1-2 tsp sugar to taste.

VARIATION
- Flavour your hot chocolate with spices (e.g. vanilla, cardamom, cinnamon, cloves,
  star anise, chilli, ginger) or grated orange or lemon zest. Strain through simmering
  basket before serving if necessary.

 5 min   10 min   easy   4 cups

Per cup:
 Energy 1042 kJ/249 kcal
Protein 7 g/Carbs 23 g/Fat 14 g

APPLE PUNCH

INGREDIENTS

500 g apple juice
500 g water
¼ cinnamon stick (3 cm)
1 star anise
50 g honey
1 tbsp dried lime blossoms or dried
  rose hips (herbal tea)
40 g lemon juice
1 orange, peeled, white pith and
  pips removed

PREPARATION

1. Place apple juice, water, cinnamon stick, star anise, honey, lime blossom tea leaves, lemon juice and orange into mixing bowl and heat **7 min/100°C/speed 1**. Allow to infuse for 15 minutes.
2. Insert simmering basket, hold it in place with spatula and strain punch into glasses or cups. Serve immediately.

 5 min 30 min  easy

6 glasses
(200 ml each)

Per glass:
Energy 303 kJ/72 kcal
Protein 0 g/Carbs 17 g/Fat 0 g

MARGARITA

INGREDIENTS

150 g Tequila

60 g orange liqueur,
(e.g. Cointreau®)

3 limes or lemons, peeled, pips
removed

100-150 g sugar

500 g ice cubes

PREPARATION

1. Place Tequila, orange liqueur, limes and sugar into mixing bowl and blend **15 sec/speed 6**.
2. Add ice cubes and blend **1 min/speed 10**. Pour margarita into glasses and serve immediately.

TIPS

- For a decorative and traditional presentation, before pouring the margarita into the glasses, rub a half lime or lemon around the rim of each glass, or turn each glass upside down and dip the rim in a plate of coloured flavoured syrup. Then dip the wet rim into a plate of salt or sugar.
- Garnish each glass with a slice of lime or lemon.

 5 min   10 min  easy 6 glasses (150 ml each)   *Per portion:*
Energy 802 kJ/192 kcal
Protein 0 g/Carbs 24 g/Fat 1 g

SANGRIA

INGREDIENTS

250 g apples, unpeeled,
   cut into pieces
1 orange
1 lemon
150 g sugar
600 g red wine
30-50 g vermouth
30-50 g brandy
30-50 g gin
¼ tsp ground cinnamon (optional)
10 ice cubes
330 g lemon soda or orange soda

USEFUL ITEMS

2 litre jug
vegetable peeler

PREPARATION

1. Place apples into mixing bowl and chop **3 sec/speed 4**.
   Transfer into a 2 litre jug and set aside.
2. With a vegetable peeler, thinly peel off the zest of one orange and
   one lemon in long strands and set aside. Remove white pith and pips
   from both citrus fruits. Place peeled orange, peeled lemon and sugar
   into mixing bowl and blend **1 min/speed 10**.
3. Add red wine, vermouth, brandy, gin, cinnamon, ice cubes and lemon
   soda and mix **30 sec/speed 2**. Transfer into jug containing chopped
   apples and serve garnished with orange and lemon zest.

TIPS

- If possible use very cold ingredients. If ingredients aren't cold, more ice cubes can
  be added into serving jug.
- You can prepare the recipe ahead of time, adding the ice cubes and soda just
  before serving.

VARIATION

- In summer, replace apples with firm ripe peaches, peeled, cut into pieces,
  and omit chopping.

 10 min   10 min    easy   6   6 glasses (200 ml each)   *Per glass:*
Energy 1162 kJ/278 kcal
Protein 1 g/Carbs 43 g/Fat 0 g

BABY FOOD

VEGETABLE-POTATO-MEAT PURÉE

INGREDIENTS

40-60 g potatoes, cut into pieces

90-100 g vegetables, cut into pieces

20-30 g meat, sinew free, cut into pieces, or fish fillet (e.g. salmon or mackerel)

400 g water

30-45 g orange juice

2-2½ tsp rapeseed oil (8-10 g)

PREPARATION

1. Place potatoes, vegetables and meat into mixing bowl, chop **3 sec/speed 5** and transfer into simmering basket.
2. Place water into mixing bowl, insert simmering basket and cook **15 min/Varoma/speed 1**.
3. Remove simmering basket with aid of spatula and transfer cooking liquid into a bowl.
4. Transfer the contents of the simmering basket into mixing bowl and add orange juice, rapeseed oil and approx. 60 g reserved cooking liquid. Purée **30 sec/speed 10**.
5. To cool purée, mix **8 min/speed 3** without measuring cup. Transfer into a bowl, check temperature is suitable for your baby and serve.

TIPS

- Select age-appropriate vegetables, meat and fish and adjust amounts according to your baby's needs.
- Adjust quantity of added cooking liquid according to desired purée consistency.

---

 10 min   35 min    easy    1 total recipe (270 g)   *Per 270 g:* Energy 831 kJ/199 kcal Protein 8 g/Carbs 14 g/Fat 12 g

CEREAL AND FRUIT PURÉE

INGREDIENTS

20 g cereal grains or rolled
　　wholemeal cereal flakes or
　　semolina
100 g fruit, cut into pieces
90 g water
1 tsp rapeseed oil (5 g)

PREPARATION

1. Place cereal grains into mixing bowl and grind **20 sec/speed 10**.
2. Add fruit and chop **3 sec/speed 5**.
3. Add water and mix **2 sec/speed 6**, then cook
   6-8 min/100°C/speed 3.
4. Add rapeseed oil and purée **10-20 sec/speed 9**, then cool purée
   6 min/speed 3 without measuring cup. Transfer into a bowl,
   check temperature is suitable for your baby and serve.

TIPS

- For the cereal to thicken the purée, it must come to the boil at least once.
- For a thicker purée, increase the amount of cereal grains or use a little less water.

 5 min　 20 min　 easy　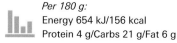 1 total recipe (180 g)

Per 180 g:
Energy 654 kJ/156 kcal
Protein 4 g/Carbs 21 g/Fat 6 g

CHAPTER INDEX

✺ easy   🍃 vegetarian

SIDE DISHES

BAKING – SAVOURY

BREADS AND ROLLS

SAUCES, DIPS AND SPREADS – SAVOURY

SAUCES, DIPS AND SPREADS – SWEET

DESSERTS AND SWEETS

BAKING – SWEET

DRINKS

BABY FOOD

ALPHABETICAL INDEX

✳ easy   🍃 vegetarian   (var.) = variation

✳ easy   🌿 vegetarian   *(var.) = variation*

✳ easy   🌿 vegetarian   *(var.) = variation*

✳ easy   🍃 vegetarian   *(var.) = variation*

T

✳ easy   🌿 vegetarian   *(var.)* = *variation*

PHOTOGRAPHY/FOOD STYLING CREDITS

All food photographs by
Photographer: Dennis Savini, Zürich,
Switzerland
Food styling: Judith Gmür-Stalder,
Sumiswald, Switzerland

With the exception of:

Pages 29, 43, 103, 105, 113, 151, 157, 165
Photographers: Silvio Posada and
Fernando Merino
Food styling: Thermomix Spain

Pages 26, 27, 57, 62, 86, 126
Photographer: D3 Studio, Nantes, France
Food styling: Emilie Laraison, Nantes,
France

Pages 37, 53, 63, 72, 78, 106
Photographer: António Nascimento,
Lisbon, Portugal
Food styling: Ana Trancoso, Lisbon,
Portugal

Pages 24, 25, 92, 160
Photographer: Craig Kinder, Perth,
Australia
Foodstyling: Natarsha Rawlins, Perth,
Australia

Pages 38, 54
Photographer: Alberto Belmont, Distrito
Federal, Mexico
Food styling: Alejandra de León, Distrito
Federal, Mexico

Pages 64, 73
Photographer: Jiří Poláček jr., Prague,
Czech Republic
Food styling: Blanka Poláčková, Prague,
Czech Republic

Pages 70, 120
Photographer: Dennis Savini, Zürich,
Switzerland
Food styling: Irène di Giacomo, Zürich,
Switzerland

Page 36
Photographer: 岑修賢, Taipei, Taiwan
Food styling: 楊環賓, Taipei, Taiwan

Page 60
Photographer/Food stylist: Małgorzata
Kujda, Wrocław, Poland

СПАСИБО · DANKE · DĚKUJI DZIĘKUJEMY · ΕΥΧΑΡΙΣΤΩ GRACIAS · GRAZIE · 谢谢 · MERCI OBRIGADO · THANK YOU

We would like to thank everyone who contributed to the success of this project, in particular the recipe developers, for all the passion and hard work they dedicated to creating and improving these recipes, as well as the testers from all over the world, for their invaluable feedback. With our appreciation for their contribution:

IMPRINT

Project responsible overall
Corinna Haase

Marketing managers
Alessandra Cattaneo, Laura Galhardo Simões, Sophie Hanon Jaure, Sandra Jossien, Magdalena Kruk-Ołpińska, Jackie van der Loon, Verena Lütke Uhlenbrock, Cécile Marié, Diane Marty, Lucie Mikesova, Jaime Porta, April Shih

Recipe development, editing and coordination
Valentina Acquilino, Miriam Aguirre, Andrea Aloe, Amy Bandy, Pavla Beníšková, Alicja Bończak, Irmgard Buth, Carla Calderón, Dagmara Dabrowska, Silvia Gherardi, Catarina Gouveia, Evelin Guder, Bonnie Hung, Renáta Koštýřová, Sylwia Kotowska, Grace McGurk, Edith Pouchard, Kami Ramini, Maria Resende, Beatriz Rodríguez Diez, Michael Tsai, Janie Turner

Project coordination
Astrid Carver Courcier, Visual Explainer, Switzerland

Nutritional values
Irmgard Buth,
NutriService GbR, Hennef, Germany

Cookbook production
Concept/Design: Lichten, Hamburg, Germany
Layout/typesetting: Effizienta oHG, Munich, Germany

Photography
People and international food photographs: Dennis Savini, Zürich, Switzerland
International food styling: Judith Gmür-Stalder, Sumiswald, Switzerland

For further photos see Photography/food styling credits, page 398

Printing
Mohn Media, Germany

Edition/Publishing
2nd edition, December 2014
16 languages

Editor
Vorwerk International Strecker & Co.
Verenastrasse 39
CH-8832 Wollerau, Switzerland

www.thermomix.com

Article number: 20541/2 en/n
Article number: 20542/2 UK
ISBN: 978-3-03844-082-6
UK-ISBN: 978-3-03844-083-3